WATCH
AND
LEARN

WATCH AND LEARN

How I Turned Hollywood Upside Down
with Netflix, Redbox, and MoviePass—
Lessons in Disruption

MITCH LOWE

hachette
BOOKS

NEW YORK

Hachette Go, an imprint of Hachette Books
Hachette Book Group
1290 Avenue of the Americas
New York, NY 10104
HachetteGo.com
Facebook.com/HachetteGo
Instagram.com/HachetteGo

First Edition: September 2022

Hachette Books is a division of Hachette Book Group, Inc.

The Hachette Go and Hachette Books name and logos are trademarks of
Hachette Book Group, Inc.

The publisher is not responsible for websites (or their content) that are not
owned by the publisher.

Print book interior design by Linda Mark.

Library of Congress Cataloging-in-Publication Data has been applied for.

ISBNs: 978-0-306-82726-6 (hardcover), 978-0-306-82728-0 (ebook)

LCCN: 2022006349

Printed in Canada

FRI

10 9 8 7 6 5 4 3 2 1

CONTENTS

FOREWORD

In the spring of 1997, out of a job and looking for something interesting to do, I pitched my friend Reed Hastings some ideas for a new company. I pitched personalized shampoo, custom dog food, subscription vitamins . . . dozens of ideas in all. But the craziest one was DVD rental by mail—an idea that everyone said would never work. "There's a Blockbuster on every corner," they would helpfully point out. "Why would anyone want to rent a movie that is going to take three or four days to arrive?"

But hope and optimism prevailed, and in April 1998 we launched the company you now know as Netflix. From there, the path we took as the company grew from its humble DVD-by-mail origins into a global entertainment company is filled with surprising stories—many of which you will hear in the following pages.

But perhaps the most surprising story of all is that when we started, none of us had the slightest idea how the video industry operated.

Well, almost none of us.

Enter Mitch Lowe, who I encountered in the summer of 1997 running a tiny booth at the Video Software Dealers Association convention in Las Vegas. It wasn't a long conversation, but he seemed to know what he was talking about, and I decided I wanted him on the team. It wasn't easy, but eventually I convinced Mitch to join us, and it ended up being one of the best decisions I ever made, as well as marking the beginning of a lifelong friendship with one of the smartest, kindest, and most interesting men I have ever met.

Initially I was drawn to him because Mitch knew video. He knew the customers, who they were, what they watched, what they liked. He knew the industry: what had been tried, what worked, what didn't. And he collected people the way some people collect Pokémon cards: he wanted a full set. Walking through a trade show with Mitch was an exercise in frustration, since almost every third person was yet another old friend that Mitch needed "just a few more minutes" to catch up with.

But as I got to know Mitch, I realized that his video industry experience was just scratching the surface. He would tell me unbelievable stories about being a club DJ in Italy, smuggling gypsy clothing out of Romania, hanging out with Andy Warhol in Monaco, dodging the military police in Egypt, and running an art gallery in San Francisco.

In the pages that follow, Mitch will share these stories with you, as well as equally surprising stories from starting Redbox and his valiant attempt to disrupt the movie ticket business with

MoviePass. But they are more than stories, they are lessons. Just as he was eager to teach *me* everything he knew about video rental, he's eager to share with you everything he's learned about business—and life.

If there's a common denominator to all his experiences, it's curiosity and experimentation, and they are traits of his that I first encountered one afternoon in the summer of 1998, not long after Netflix had launched. "I've got an idea," Mitch blurted out, sticking his head into my office. "I just read that Bill Clinton's testimony in the Monica Lewinsky affair is going to be publicly released. I wonder if we can make our own DVD of the footage?"

"Mitch," I countered, "do you know anything about how you're going to get that content? Or about mastering DVDs? In fact, is that even a thing?"

Then he gave me a look that I would see hundreds of times over the next several years. "No," he somewhat sheepishly answered. "But I'll bet I can figure it out."

And off he went to do just that. None of us—least of all Mitch—could have anticipated the events that followed, as a project he thought would take a day or two stretched into several sleepless weeks, with dozens of dead ends, false trails, and forced errors (including mistakenly shipping a porn DVD to a few hundred surprised customers). But Mitch delivered, and not only was it the public relations event that put Netflix on the map, but it laid the groundwork for the coming decades of trial and error.

Over the coming years, Mitch and I worked together on dozens of crazy projects, all of which were best described as the ones that everybody said would never work. And after our last Netflix project together, when I spent the summer of 2002 with Mitch in

Las Vegas trying to help him launch a Netflix kiosk, I thought I had seen the last of Mitch's *"I'll figure it out"* ideas.

I should have known better.

Ten years later, in the fall of 2013 when he reached me by phone, I knew immediately that Mitch had found another one. "You've got to meet these guys," he blurted out excitedly. "They've got a company called MoviePass that's doing a subscription service for movie theaters." And with that, I once again found myself alongside Mitch working on another idea that everyone said would never work. I didn't last long there, and I won't spoil the ending here, but the eight-year adventure in category disruption that followed is one of the most fascinating and colorful business stories ever, and as usual, Mitch was right in the center of it.

Whether you're just starting out in business or already have a long track record of success, you'll find plenty to learn from a man who has seen it all, done most of it, and met everyone. You'll see . . . there's nobody else like Mitch.

MARC RANDOLPH

Cofounder and first CEO of Netflix and
best-selling author of *That Will Never Work:
The Birth of Netflix and the Amazing Life of an Idea*

[1]

A HELL OF A RIDE

Eightfold Path
Our births, learning to stand, and all our ups and downs reflect
that the true way to success is not a straight path from A to
B. Neither is coming to terms with who we are or why we are
here on this earth.

I was there for all of it. The total disruption of the movie and TV
business. I not only had a ringside seat, I had a role in shaping
the way we consume entertainment. And through this evolution I
witnessed the stubborn resistance to real innovation and the epic
arrogance of some entertainment executives toward that process.

In the end, all my colleagues and I had going for us was intuition, perseverance, and an unerring sense of what the viewing
customer really wanted—a sense, I might add, that the very people
who sold and distributed those TV series and movies not always
but often lacked. Either that, or they were just too shortsighted to
care, and way too careful to protect their reliable revenue streams.

The stories I could tell . . . well, that's why this book exists.
To tell those stories that are instructive to inspiring innovation

and helpful in becoming a better leader. But there's more to it than that. I want you to understand how we got from movies and TV shows released and controlled rigidly by the huge studios to a world where we can stream whatever we want on our big screens at home, sitting on the couch with popcorn we made ourselves, or watching a smartphone while waiting at a bus stop. I want you to know what it took to disrupt a huge and hidebound business—and the lessons you can draw from that story for your own quixotic adventures, whether that means upending uninspired management at your company or disrupting whatever business domain *you* have your dreams set on.

What's in this book? I'll show you how I went from being a high school dropout smuggling cheap money into Eastern Europe and transporting used Mercedes sedans to Damascus to being the owner of a chain of video stores. I'll explain how, as the "video guy" who knew the rental business, I joined up with Reed Hastings and Marc Randolph to be a founding senior executive at Netflix, a company that built a tight monthly relationship with movie renters via the internet and the postal service when everyone else thought you could only do that with expensive stores on Main Street in every town. I'll show you how, in my quest to demonstrate that I could manage things at a big company, I helped McDonald's build a billion-dollar DVD kiosk business, and how we spun that out to create Redbox, the DVD rental business that's outlived Blockbuster and all the rest. And finally, I'll explain how I tried to remake the theatrical exhibition business with MoviePass, a monthly subscription to the movies that, even as it failed, still managed to change the way theaters operate, a change that is still reverberating in the COVID era.

Along the way, a need for a renewed sense of work/life balance led me to spend time at a meditation center and renewed my teenage adoption of Buddhism. I've told these stories with reference to zen principles that I have adopted in my life since then. These are the principles that have guided me as I have navigated the venal world of entertainment and communed with the desires of the millions who consume it. These principles have also helped put the greater arc of my life's journey and career into perspective—I start each chapter with one of them, including the elements of the Eightfold Path to begin Chapters 2 through 9. They were developed thousands of years ago and over time were as good a plan as I needed. The Eightfold Path has served me as a structure but not as dogma or religion, only a very well-thought-out direction. These principles are the reason I see myself as the zen disruptor.

People think disruption has to be about violent upheaval. It doesn't. More often than not, it's more about constant pressure. Like drops of water wearing away at stone, a zen disruptor's approach generates success slowly but inexorably, creating a long-term triumph over the rigid thinking of traditional companies in sclerotic industries. If you understand the customers better—and if you have the imagination to find new ways of giving those customers what they want—you will always win. It may take many years, it may take more than one try, and you may fail more often than you would like. But industries that are arrogant and fail to innovate always collapse eventually—and a zen disruptor is there to remake the business when they do.

In my story I will share many lessons I have learned along the way. Perhaps some can help you. Before quitting high school in the middle of my senior year, I realized that learning goes on forever, and whatever you learn along the way can last a lifetime. Since then I have seen that lessons can come from anywhere, and often from an unexpected source. It may be witnessing how people respond to failure, or how founders and execs respond when the company is about to collapse, or even the way seabirds fly low over the breaking waves. Or, occasionally, from teachers and public speakers like me.

Even now, in my late sixties, I feel as healthy and vibrant as I did in my forties. I go to bed almost every night feeling as if I have done what I needed to do that day, and I wake up excited the next morning. I make sure of that by moving anything important I did not do that day onto a future date. It's a great way to remove stress.

In this story you will see that as often as I have succeeded, I have also failed. My undying positive interpretation of everything from people to ideas to plans has opened many opportunities for adventure. It has also gotten me involved with people and businesses that were at best bad ideas and at worst conniving plots. While I was often saddened, hurt, and angry, I would not trade those bad times for anything. Throughout my life I have learned never to burn bridges. I have experienced over and over again how someone I never wanted to see again has come back into my life for the better.

I have traveled and lived in foreign countries and all over the United States. I moved with my parents and my wonderful brother, Mark, from Omaha, Nebraska, to La Mesa, California, in 1957, to follow my dad's work as an aeronautic engineer. I ended up going to nine different schools and learned to make the best of being in new surroundings. The downside is that as a kid I had few friends. I took off to Canada while a junior in high school, on an adven-

4

ture that we thought could lead almost anywhere in the world with my friend Kirk, then moved to Germany to live with my dad, got kicked out of the house after I brought home some vagrant travelers I met in Munich, and lived in Italy, France, Spain, Israel, and Monaco—as I'll describe in the next chapter. In the United States, I have lived in the San Francisco Bay Area, Chicago, New York, and Miami. I have been living in Mexico since before COVID and continue to travel.

This story will track the three building blocks of entertainment distribution through my own experiences in helping to disrupt them. It starts with retail entertainment in the proliferating video stores from the 1980s. It continues with the DVDs that enabled Netflix to build a "movies by mail" subscription service and Redbox to create a DVD vending kiosk network that grew to almost $2 billion in annual revenue. And it segues into the streaming world that has changed everything about the way we think about and consume media. In the last chapter I will share my perspective on the future and where this is all going.

I hope you enjoy my stories as much as I have enjoyed telling them, and living through them.

THE BUSINESS AND ART
OF RECKLESS ABANDON

Samma Vayama (Right Effort)
Our efforts should be significant enough and sustained enough
to accomplish what we are trying to achieve.

My early adulthood was a time of calculated reckless abandon. Reckless because I would try almost anything. But calculated because every one of those reckless decisions seemed worth doing.

Unlike most of the successful entrepreneurs and business-people you hear about, I never went to college, and I didn't even finish high school. While they were learning from professors, I was learning by trying, and often failing at, just about anything you could imagine.

I had to make friends quickly and try out new experiences, because things were rarely stable in my childhood. I went to nine different schools between first grade and high school; in third grade, I went to three in one year. I never had much time to make friends or learn how to be one. Instead, I spent my time reading and contemplating. I was a planner and a schemer, always gaming things out in my mind.

A lot of who I am is a result of what I did as a teenager. This period in my life, starting in the mid-sixties, was characterized by an unfettered and wide-ranging curiosity. If it looked interesting, I was willing to try it, since I was both a bit lazy in those days about analyzing the pros and cons of decisions, and heck I was young and naïvely felt invincible. I wanted to know how the world worked, how people interacted, what business and selling were all about. And I was curious about places far from my home in Northern California. With all the moving and the lack of friends, I had to be self-motivated.

My earliest search for enlightenment meant escaping from the reality my parents had planned for me—school, graduating, holding down a job, figuring out how to make money. Instead, my mind naturally expanded as I was exposed to the most diverse possible group of people. The more people I met, the more I craved interaction with lots of different kinds of people. I learned there was no right and wrong way to be, just different perspectives. The Zen Buddhist way of life includes taking everything in, observing it, and figuring out what you want to take and what you want to leave behind.

As I'll describe, by the time I was eighteen, I'd visited a dozen different countries and done jobs from disco club DJ to smuggling currency behind the Iron Curtain to stealing bananas and grapefruit from Arabs in a war zone. The people I met were incredible, and many of them went on to become famous cultural and countercultural figures, from beat poets like Gary Snyder to artists like Andy Warhol. That open attitude about people and things has a lot to do with how I approach business—always from an attitude of intense curiosity, and always tinkering with things to see how they work.

The other thing that led to these experiences was girls. I fall in love very quickly. I would see a girl and instantly want to be with her. A lot of guys may feel this way, but most don't do anything about it. In the sixties, there were lots of girls with the same attitude, and I ended up making friends with and going to bed with a bunch of them. So in many ways, the story of my teen years is a story of a lot of girlfriends and the adventures we had together.

My first business enterprise was born in Santa Clara when I was eleven years old. I had received a science kit for Christmas. I applied what I had learned reading *Scientific American* and built a chemical magic show program. I told my brother, Mark, that I thought we could make some money by selling tickets at twenty-five cents a pop to neighbors for a show in our carport. We bought a roll of tickets and spent the next few days knocking on the door of every condo in the development. We sold around $20 or $25 worth, which was a gold mine. It helped that we said a portion of the money would go to the Red Cross. I'm not sure whether that was my idea or Mark's, but I suppose now I owe them a few bucks.

By the time I was in high school, we were living with my mom and my third stepfather, Ted Bekins, who was from a very wealthy family in the moving and storage business. We were in Mill Valley, California, north of San Francisco on the far side of the Golden Gate Bridge. Mom was divorced. She let me do pretty much whatever I wanted, for the most part. I went to a small private high school in San Francisco, the Urban School, which in those days had an open education model, which meant, essentially, no attendance requirements. That was the start of making my own rules, starting with a hitchhiking trip in the summer after my junior year.

My brother's friend and I had this idea to use the summer of 1968 to hitchhike to Canada. In our fantasy we imagined we would then hitchhike across Canada to Nova Scotia, where we would find a private plane to hitch a ride on to Europe and then who knows what. (As you can see, the calculation part of my calculated reckless abandon wasn't very precisely tuned.) With that plan and $45 in my pocket and a hefty $90 in my friend's, we started off on our journey north.

We were on Highway 101 near the Oregon border with our thumbs out for rides. Around dusk a beaten-down red pickup truck screeched to a halt. A beautiful, slender blond girl, barefoot and in shorts, yelled out the window to us, "Hey, you guys!" She said she was going in our direction about thirty miles to her cabin and if we wanted a ride and even a place to crash, we could stay at her place.

My fellow traveler shared a sly glance with me. Then we piled our backpacks and sleeping bags in the back of her truck and were off. She told us that her boyfriend was up in Oregon picking fruit, and she would take us the next day. Obviously, we were happy to get a ride that far north and thrilled to be with a self-confident and sexy woman who was a few years older than us. We got to her place and after we shared a meal, she startled us by saying she wanted to sleep with one of us, and she would decide who. In my head I was probably like a kid in class raising my hand and yelling, "Pick me, pick me," and she did. He was annoyed. It was a momentous night in the life of a soon-to-be sixteen-year-old.

The next day we headed out going up the coast. An hour into the drive she decided that she and I would jump in a sleeping bag in the back while Kirk drove. He was a terrible driver, and she and I were oblivious to the danger we were in as he weaved back and forth on the road and eventually nearly ran out of gas.

We got to Seaside, Oregon, that night, and my adolescent dream was over as she threw her arms around her boyfriend. Kirk and I went on our way. That was a pretty good start to my plan of calculated reckless abandon.

We made it to Vancouver, Canada. I started interning for an underground newspaper there called the *Georgia Straight*. Walking along the shore at English Bay, I met a girl named Juli. We instantly connected. She had quit school just before that. She and I ran away for a while to Vancouver Island. A few weeks later I snuck her back into the United States using an ID belonging to the older sister of a friend of a friend.

It was amazing that the St. Louis, Missouri, driver's license for an eighteen-year-old girl passed as ID for Juli, who was a young looking fifteen-year-old—you can't get away with that these days.

Anyway, we ended up hiding out at the house of the beat poet Gary Snyder in the hills of Mill Valley. Juli's parents sent the Canadian Mounties to track us down. Eventually, my mom and stepdad found us.

Both sets of parents agreed to an idea I suggested, which was that we meet with a family counselor in San Rafael, California. I'm still not sure why my parents went along with that. We explained our position, which was that Juli had quit school and was not going back and had entered the United States illegally, and

I wasn't going back to school either. We were both now living in Gary Snyder's house.

Both sets of parents were concerned. The counselor presented a solution that we all agreed to. Juli's parents would rent the extra bedroom in my mom's house, and Juli would attend the public high school, Mt. Tamalpais, while I would return to the Urban School. I think the only reason they all agreed is that Juli's parents were older and a bit worn down; she was their fourth child, with a huge gap in years between her and the third child.

My recollection is that I was a really good student in the classes that I loved: history, math, and philosophy. Memory can be a tricky thing, as I was to learn, and not just for me. At my forty-year high school reunion, my class had only twelve students, and nobody remembered who I was. Eventually they said, "Oh, you were the kid who never showed up for school." While I loved the classes, I didn't do the work. I got lots of Ds accompanied by comments like "Great potential if he would only apply himself." So much for doing well in classes I loved. Ds all around.

I felt like I wasn't learning anything important or anything that I would use in my life. I became fascinated with Buddhism, originally after reading books such as *Siddhartha* by Hermann Hesse and *Magic Mountain* by Thomas Mann. Reading offered me answers to the deeper meanings in life because I just felt lost. I was motivated by the desire to get out into the world and experience it and learn what was going on.

One day, I went to Juli's high school to pick her up, just as I usually did. She wasn't where I was supposed to pick her up and when I went around the corner, I saw her making out with this guy named Rob. The pain and the jealousy was more than I could handle, and that was it for that relationship.

At that point I decided I should drop out. Surprisingly, my mother embraced the idea and offered to help. She introduced me to a guy named Funky Sam, who in the daytime was a lawyer in Sausalito and by night a publisher of those infamous black light posters featuring rock concerts, the Kama Sutra, and Disney's seven dwarves in lewd positions under Snow White's skirt. I had the feeling Sam was trying to have an affair with my mom and that if he could get me out of the way, that would clear a path for his advances.

"Why don't you become our European salesman?" asked Sam. He knew I had had enough of school and that I'd be willing to go to Europe, since my father lived in Munich.

My attitude about that trip to Europe sort of followed from another Thomas Mann book I'd read, *Confessions of Felix Krull, Confidence Man*. Krull's story took place in the twenties. He was bright and quick and good-looking, and just went from one crazy thing to another, pretending he was a doctor, for example. I just felt like, what was the difference between him and me, nothing more than a couple of years of education, and I could learn fast.

So I was ready to try anything. Funky Sam bundled me up with a big roll of sample posters and order forms. I worked with a couple of my teachers on projects I would do while traveling that they said could qualify me to graduate. When I got on that flight from San Francisco to Europe, I felt total freedom for the first time. I was an adult now and I had no one else to rely on, and it really gave me a sense of pride.

As soon as I got to Germany, I started looking for poster companies that might buy from me. These were still the days when there was a huge US military presence in Germany and almost everyone spoke English. With the exchange rate, Germany was inexpensive. You could buy a car for less than $5,000 and food was really cheap. My first sale was to a retail bookstore chain in Frankfurt that bought $100,000 worth of black light posters. My commission was 20 percent, so here I was, suddenly with $20,000 in 1970 in Europe, which was a fortune. Instead of sitting in a high school classroom, I was thinking that I was on a roll. I loved this whole idea of making a sale and earning my cut.

Unfortunately, about a month later, Disney sued the company over the Snow White poster, Funky Sam's most popular item, and he had to fold up shop.

Later on in my career, I'd have many other experiences with legal challenges and violations of intellectual property rights leading to ruined businesses. But at the time, I was a seventeen-year-old high school dropout in Germany with money burning a hole in my pocket. I was ready to set out and see Europe, and I feared nothing.

I bought an old BMW police motorcycle and rode it down to Positano in southern Italy. I spent time sitting in cafés along the beach staring listlessly out at all the interesting people walking by. After I'd bummed around for a week, a young woman, tattooed from head to foot including her face, sat at my café table and introduced herself as Vali. She later turned out to be another of those people I had just bumped into who later became well known. She ended up palling around with famous artists and writers like Salvador Dali and Tennessee Williams and being the star of a documentary titled *The Witch of Positano*.

Vali enchanted me with stories of her life traveling all over Europe and Morocco. On a whim, she offered me a slot as a DJ at the local disco. For the second time in less than six months I took on a job where I had no clue what I was doing. I am sure that I was a terrible DJ, but it was loud and the people were having fun and they didn't much care. Jobs like that would become a recurring theme throughout my life: I always had this desire to challenge myself with roles that I had no experience in.

The summer was just beginning, and with school out Juli contacted me and wondered if I would want to travel around Europe with her. I was still hurting but missed her as well, and well heck, it would be fun for a couple of months.

Juli and I traveled around Europe in a BMW 500. You might think that is a motorcycle, and you would be half right. It was a cheap small car powered by a motorcycle engine. We went to Paris, London, the northern tip of Scotland, back to France, and down to the north of Spain. Then we rode over to the Italian Riviera and up to Switzerland, where we met her mother. Her mother wanted to take us to Israel, where her family were big supporters of the Labor Party. She wanted to give us kind of a VIP view of Israel.

We stayed at the finest hotels, and we ate at great restaurants. We also saw the beautiful work taking place on the kibbutzim. The kibbutzim were collective farms established by the Israelis in parts of Israel that had been occupied after the wars—they were part agricultural outpost, part collectivist experiment, and part geopolitical strategy to solidify Israeli presence in these border areas. The people working in the kibbutzim were called kibbutzniks.

While we were visiting the kibbutzim, Juli became enamored by the people there, especially the women in the Israeli military.

Coming from the San Francisco Bay Area in the sixties, we were Vietnam War protesters and antimilitary, so I found this feeling really counter to all that we believed in. But of course, Juli was Jewish, so what the hell did I know about what was important to her. I found her attitude kind of superficial, especially when she told me she wanted to buy a woman's military uniform to wear; I thought, how could you be so disingenuous to be antiwar and then want to wear a military uniform as a fashion statement.

I think I felt a little hemmed in with Juli and her mom in a strange country with their unfamiliar attitudes toward it. I felt a need to be a little more genuine. So I boldly, if naïvely, stated, "Well if you really believe in Israel, you should stay and fight for the country." She told me she planned to go back to the United States to finish high school. It was once again time for me to try something new and show the adults what I was made of. I said, "Well, then I am going to stay and fight." Her mother was glad to get me away from her, so she decided to make my statement come true. She said she had some friends that could get me into a border kibbutz.

Before I knew it, I was on a bus to a kibbutz called Ashdot Yaakov Ichud, which was founded back in the 1920s by Zionists who came and bought the land from Arabs. It was right on the Israeli border, south of the Sea of Galilee, alongside two rivers— the Jordan River and the Yarmuk River—which forms the border between Syria and Jordan. This region is verdant and beautiful. You wake up in the morning and the air is soft and warm and you see banana fields and grapefruit trees everywhere.

The Golan Heights were about twenty miles away. Israel had recently taken the Golan Heights from the Syrians, because the

Syrians had been lobbing rockets down on the farms below. Just before I got there, a farmer and his son had been killed while opening an irrigation ditch on a nearby kibbutz. A member of the Palestinian Fatah faction had attached a World War II antivehicle mine to the wheel of an irrigation control, where it exploded and killed them. The children in the kibbutz slept underground for safety, and we would have air-raid drills from time to time.

One of the first things that happens when you get to the kibbutz is that they identify special skills you might have that could be employed on the farm. I told them that I used to spend every summer on my grandparents' farm outside Omaha, so I knew how to drive a John Deere tractor—and they had a bunch of those.

But their John Deere tractors were armored and they had steel cockpits with bulletproof windows. As a driver, every morning at three a.m. I would hitch a heavy sled to the back of the tractor and drag the sled along the dirt farm roads to see if land mines had been planted in the road overnight. Luckily, nothing ever blew up while I was driving.

One day, we were told to prepare one of the tractors with a flatbed trailer and be prepared to cross into Jordan to harvest grapefruit. Shortly after that we heard jet fighters going over our heads and flying low above a farm village across the border in Jordan. The Israelis knew that after a fighter jet run, the farm village would be deserted. We were instructed to cross over into Jordan and quickly harvest as many bananas and grapefruits as we could and bring them back to our side.

A month or so later there was a rocket attack. A few volunteers and I were on the second floor of an unfinished building. We didn't hear the alarm, which is meant to notify you to go underground.

When we heard an explosion, I panicked and instead of doing the right thing and going down the steps into the shelter, I jumped off the unfinished balcony. I ended up badly hurting my knee. They took me to the Hadassah hospital in Jerusalem to recover.

My reckless abandon was still pretty reckless, but I started calculating what to do next. I'd had enough of living on a kibbutz. After the swelling had gone down, I decided I would explore Israel. I hitchhiked to Be'er Sheva, then to Eilat on the Gulf of Aqaba, and then down to a beautiful crescent bay in the Sinai Peninsula called Nuweiba (at this time Israel occupied the Sinai Peninsula and years later gave it back to Egypt), camping out along the way. Traveling around Israel at that time in 1970, I saw an amazing people fighting to build a country. They weren't just building up a military force, they were building huge value in infrastructure and knowledge and training and education and business. They were building a country almost from scratch in a very inhospitable environment. I saw firsthand how a small number of people working together, focused on a clear mission and on a long-term goal, can change their world. It gave me an amazing amount of confidence in people, and I think it had a lot to do with how I looked at being an entrepreneur later in my life.

At the same time, I thought, who are these Arabs and Palestinians on the other side that are doing everything possible to destroy Israel and to kill people? I thought, what is it that's causing probably good people to hate other good people? I vowed at that point that I would try to go to the other side, to Syria and Jordan and Lebanon and Egypt, and try to understand what was motivating people to do such awful and evil things to each other. As I'll describe a few pages from now, I did end up doing business in

Syria, Lebanon, and Egypt and learning about the people, who were ready to do business just like anyone else.

Juli had gone back to California to finish high school, which left me to decide what's next. The next step in my calculated reckless abandon was to learn a language, and French seemed the most romantic, so I went to Paris. By this time all that money I had made from my one poster sale and the measly pay at the disco in Positano was running low. In Paris I found a room with a sink in the Saint-Germain area, just a block from the Seine, for eleven francs a day, which I think was less than $3 a night. After signing up for French classes at the Berlitz school on Rue de Montparnasse, I once again started looking for work. At this point I was living off a pint of plain yogurt drenched in honey and a loaf of French bread each day.

During this half year or so I remember my dad and younger brother coming to find me—or in their view, rescue me, since they noted I was down to a skeletal 150 or so pounds from my normal weight of 180. Always the romantic, I fell in love with a beautiful dark-haired French girl, and we made the best of every moment she could steal away from school and her parents. One day there was a note from her slipped under the door of my room saying her father had found out she was sleeping with a long-haired American hippie and that I better leave town quickly as he was "coming after me." Not wasting any time, I felt like this was a good cue to find a new adventure. I had gotten my motorcycle out of storage and had it all ready to travel, with my sleeping bag and tent attached to the rear.

Calculated reckless abandon told me it was time to leave. But where to go?

I had recently learned from my brother that a girl named Judy from back in Mill Valley was going to school for a year along the coast north of Barcelona. I'd always found this girl incredibly hot. She hardly knew my name, but at this point I was gaining more and more confidence and thought, why don't I go find her. All I knew was that she was going to a small private school in a Catalan town called Blanes. Blanes was a couple of days south on my motorcycle, so there I went.

When I think about my good fortune in what happened next, it feels like I must have done something right in some previous life. I rode into the beachside village of Blanes at around three in the afternoon. The street along the water was lined with cafés and restaurants. I saw a bunch of high school kids hanging out in a small café with an open outdoor patio. I pulled up, dusted off all the road dirt, and sat down. A couple girls were speaking English, so I asked if they knew a girl named Judy. I was floored when they said, "Oh yeah, she will be here in a little bit."

I learned that she had gotten into some trouble and was in a sort of after-school detention. Not much later, she turned up. Instead of asking, "What are you doing here?" she opened with "Is that your bike?" And then off we went. We went back to the tiny place she shared with another girl, she stuffed her clothes in a bag, and we took off to Barcelona, which was about fifty miles south, never to return.

After a week or so in a hotel in Barcelona we discovered that everyone was headed to the island of Ibiza, so we hopped on a ferry. Today, Ibiza is a bustling tourist island, but in 1970, I don't think there were any big hotels. We found a little farmhouse—a *finka*—in the middle of a fig and olive orchard that rented for $45 a month.

We shared the rent with three other bikers from the Carolinas. Of course there was no running water and no electricity.

It was an idyllic life. The Mediterranean water was azure green and crystal clear. There were small hidden beaches you could get to by scrambling down steep rocks or swim to from some more accessible spot. Every day, we would explore different parts of the island. On the other side of the island there was a beautiful, secluded little bay with rocks sticking out where you could jump twenty or thirty feet down into the water. We had to swim around a projecting point of rocks to get to this little beach.

We arrived with bottles of beer and lunch and we were having a great time. We were all very careful—at first. If you jumped straight down you would hit the rocks below, so to be safe you had to run and leap out far. Pretty soon the big brown bottles of San Miguel beer started having an effect, and the bikers started challenging each other to jump backward. One took the bait and ended up smashing his legs on the rocks. Now we had an emergency, and we all had to go in the water and swim him around the point, dragging him along. We got him up to a nearby nunnery, where they cleaned him up and then brought him to the hospital.

Once he was taken care of, Judy and I jumped on my BMW. She was holding a liter-size bottle of beer in each hand, with both of us in swimsuits and sandals. Despite our friend getting hurt, life was great, couldn't be better. But then I went a bit too fast rounding a turn, hit some gravel, and lost control of the bike. Judy and I slid along the pavement. The road rubbed my forearms and knees bloody. Sliding behind me, Judy broke one bottle into the palm of her hand, the glass gashing her so that she was bleeding profusely. Miraculously, she saved the second bottle. What a girl! That came in handy; once we recovered our senses, she cracked that one open and used the beer to clean and sterilize our wounds.

I have never forgotten what I learned that day. When everything is going perfectly and you don't have a care in the world is exactly when you need to pay extra attention. My observation from that point on was that when you felt the most secure and safe was when most shit happened. It is easy to drop your guard and get hurt. In fact, all my life since then, when things seem too good to be true, I remind myself of that day.

We were done with Ibiza—it was time to take my reckless abandon tour somewhere else.

We then decided to drive across southern Europe to Greece. We traveled along the Côte d'Azur in France, took a side trip to the islands of Corsica and Sardinia, and then took a ferry to mainland Italy. We traveled across Italy to Venice and down to what is today the coast of Croatia, and then hit the Albanian border, but Albania was off-limits to Westerners at the time. Going around Albania we passed thru Pec, a mountain town in what was at the time Yugoslavia (now it's in Kosovo). The men in those towns all wore white hats that looked like eggshells. It was very strange.

Finally, our luck ran out. Our BMW motorcycle had been breaking down over the last couple weeks, and now in the middle of nowhere the spring controlling the spinning generator broke and was unrepairable without somehow getting it fifty miles or so back to the nearest town. We had had it with the bike and thought that hitchhiking the rest of the way to Greece made more sense.

Judy and I were conveniently alongside a cliff and I couldn't stop thinking about all those movies where they push a vehicle off and it bounces down and then has this big explosion. That seemed like a cool idea and a fitting way to say goodbye to a friend that took us almost all the way across Europe. So, with a heave, off it went, down, down, down, then rolling over and then . . . silence. It just kind of crumpled at the bottom. Life is not like the movies.

That ending taught me two things. One is that at a certain point, you have to give up on trying to make something work: cut your losses. Years later, making some of my riskiest business decisions, I wish I had remembered that lesson. That moment also taught me that no matter how big your expectations are, you will very likely end up disappointed, or that things won't come to fruition as you expect they will. As one of the Buddhist dogmas says, life is full of pain and suffering, and human desire causes this suffering.

We hitchhiked our way on the backs of trucks and in a car or two and made our way from Yugoslavia to Greece. We spent time on some of the islands, and we heard that there was an inexpensive cruise ship heading out of Piraeus, the harbor for Athens, to Alexandria, Egypt. There we saw unimaginable things, in sites that today are almost impossible for tourists to see. For example, in the Valley of the Kings we visited Tutankhamen's tomb with just one guide and no protective rails or shields covering the priceless wall paintings.

After a few weeks we decided to head back to Europe and then home to the States. But that wasn't going to be easy. We found a ship leaving Alexandria to Istanbul and arrived there with something like $90 total between us. We had to get to Munich, Germany, to see if my dad could loan us some money—this was all, of course, before the internet, before cell phones, before credit and debit cards. Judy's parents were super angry at us by this point and not willing to help.

So we decided we had to hitchhike our way to Germany, and we couldn't afford hotels. The first truck that picked us up on the outskirts of Istanbul was headed through Bulgaria and into Romania, both hard communist police states behind the Iron Curtain. It made a big impact on me to see Romania, a country of European-looking people living as if it were the 1800s. In the mountains there were few cars; most people got around on horse-drawn carts. People walked from their houses up and down the mountains into town. I noticed the colorful traditional clothing of hand-embroidered and beaded blouses and fur-trimmed vests and jackets. It seemed almost haute couture to my hippie sense of style. We saw too that the black market exchange rate in Romania made buying cultural items like silk blouses incredibly inexpensive — less than $20 for an embroidered silk blouse that probably had taken two hundred hours to make. I sensed a business opportunity.

When the truck dropped us off in the early evening in the Romanian capital of Bucharest, we walked for a few minutes and spotted a small worker's-style restaurant. Outside we promised each other that we would go in and not leave until we had found someone to give us a place to sleep for the night, before hitchhiking on to Germany the following day. I am not sure where that kind of naïve confidence came from but after a couple of hours, two guys who said they were night watchmen at an under-construction apartment building offered us a place to sleep. It was a dingy room with a thin mattress, but we fell asleep right away. In hindsight I can't believe that nothing bad happened to us or that the people we met were actually so kind.

Unfortunately, the next morning when we awoke, I discovered that I had been bitten by something, maybe a spider. My eyes and one entire side of my face were swollen, and I had a rash covering my whole body. We knew no one would pick us up with that zombie look, so we headed to a park bench and waited and waited for the swelling to go down. There was no thought of a doctor and not enough money to waste on one. By late afternoon the swelling was half down and we decided to splurge half of our $90 on two train tickets as far through Romania as $45 would get us, which was a city called Cluj-Napoca. This was not far from the Hungarian border and on a major road heading toward Vienna and on to Germany.

We made it to Germany and with help from our parents, we got back home. Soon we were renting a small place from Judy's parents in Stinson Beach, California. But our romance was not going to last long once we were back. Judy's interest strayed to other guys. We broke up and I left with everything I owned in a couple of grocery bags.

Any normal person would have ended the adventuring. But my calculations and my reckless abandon intersected each other once again. While I had no education, no real skills, and no prospects, I remembered the Romanian blouses. So I borrowed $5,000 from my mother, went to Romania, bought Romanian clothes, then brought them back and sold them on Rodeo Drive in Beverly Hills for a hundred times what I paid.

After a while, I developed a lucrative three-stop model of travel, buying, and selling that didn't get me rich but paid the bills. It started by flying to Heidelberg, Germany, where I would purchase a used Mercedes diesel car. I'd then head east. My first stop was either in Zurich, Switzerland, or Vienna, Austria, where I would go to local banks and buy $10,000 or $15,000 worth of Romanian money. I would pay roughly one one-hundredth of the official rate in country, which was established by the corrupt government of Nicolae Ceauşescu. The biggest challenge, besides importing money being illegal, was that the largest bill was the 100-lei note, which cost me around $3. That meant I had to hide 3,000 to 5,000 bills when I traveled.

My father, who spent many years behind the Iron Curtain sourcing info on Russian and other Eastern European aviation technologies, told me once that the last place customs will look is on your person. I didn't ask how he knew that, but it made perfect sense. So what I would do is buy extra-large hiking boots for me and a companion and we would put three inches of bills under each foot and get used to walking on those shoes a couple days before crossing the border.

Once in Romania, we would buy Romanian women's silk embroidered blouses, fur-trimmed vests, and other items from farm girls' dowries. Next, we would drive through Bulgaria to Greece and ship the items to the United States. Then we would head on across Turkey to Syria, where we would sell the cars to taxi companies. Finally, we'd take a flight to Cairo, where we would buy old Roman glass and appliquéd awnings, and then head back to California to sell everything.

For the next couple of years, about every two or three months I would gather up money from the sales from previous trips and plan my next buying trip. I did that eighteen times over the course of ten years.

For each trip this was between $15,000 and $20,000, which in Heidelberg was enough to purchase a 1960s Mercedes 230 or 250 diesel and acquire enough Romanian currency in Zurich or Vienna and make the purchasing tour profitable. I saw each of these adventures as a good excuse to invite a recent girlfriend, or in one case a girl I hoped would become my girlfriend, along with me.

On one of these trips where the romantic relationship did not work out and the girl I was with returned on her own to California, I met a girl named Patty in Munich who was an aspiring singer, the daughter of Americans living in Germany. She and I had a torrid affair and soon I asked her to return with me to the United States, where we would get an apartment and she would become my partner selling the Romanian blouses. We got an apartment on Miller Avenue in Mill Valley, and with her salesmanship, our sales took off. Things were going great until one day she surprised me and asked me, did I love her? This would be one of the many times in my life that I would respond before thinking more and being sensitive to someone else's feelings. It was a great lesson and while I did not learn it for many years after, it serves as a reminder of how stupid I can be. Not thinking, I said, "No, I don't love you." Within thirty minutes she had packed her stuff and left, never to return or contact me again. I later learned that she had become a quite popular punk rock performer in San Francisco singing under the name of Pearl E. Gates.

In early 1973 I returned from a one-month buying trip and was picked up at the San Francisco airport by my mother and her longtime boyfriend Roger. It was 6:30 a.m. and she informed me that—surprise, surprise—I had an appointment at the Oakland Army induction center to determine if I was physically fit for the draft. In those last years of the Vietnam War, the draft was a lottery. Each day of the year was given a random number between 1 and 365. They would call up people starting with number 1 and typically get to 100 or so before the quota was filled. In 1973 I was number 46 and so highly likely to be drafted. As a war protester with experience overseas where I saw how naïve and wrong some of the US foreign policy was, I looked for options to avoid the draft.

My mother had found a psychologist who wrote me a conscientious objector evaluation, which my mother brought with her to the airport. The Army induction center was just as you have seen in movies—fill out paperwork, show ID, and get undressed down to your underwear along with forty or so other young men standing around waiting for direction. Doctors were checking each person, eyes, throat, and reflexes, and then it was on to the psychologist. I had put the letter in my white briefs and pulled it out for the doctor. Ten minutes later I had received a six-month deferral; with total relief I exited the center so my mom could drive me back to Mill Valley.

Two buying trips later, imagine my surprise when I received in the mail an induction letter telling me to report for the Army in a matter of a couple of weeks. I was shocked because I had assumed I would get another chance to talk my way out of this using the letter from the psychologist. That was not to be.

Within a week I had stored all my belongings, moved out of my apartment, and left my forwarding address as my brother's place on the other side of Mill Valley, and I was on a flight to France.

My dad and his wife had moved from Munich, Germany, where he ran a subscription-based newsletter aimed at aeronautic engineers called *The Munich Letter*, to Cap Martin, a town situated between Monaco and the Italian border. He lived in a house next to the orchard where Winston Churchill spent some of his last days painting. Through a friend of a friend they found me an apartment, the ground floor of a furnished two-bedroom house with gardens, smack in the middle of Monte Carlo, rent-protected for a whopping $160 a month. It had a beautiful view of the sea and the first hairpin turns on the Grand Prix racetrack, just down the street from the Café de Paris and the Monte Carlo Casino.

My prime location also made me an attractive friend to all kinds of celebrities and the children of big businesspeople. There was Bruno Robalo, whose family owned the company that made the seats for all the Fiat factories, and Ellen D'Estainville, or should I say Countess D'Estainville, who owned the first block of the Champs-Élysées. I also befriended Regine, who was the face of Jimmy's, a club with locations in Paris and New York as well as one in Monte Carlo.

It was during this time in Monte Carlo that I met Federico De Laurentiis, the son of the famous Italian director Dino De Laurentiis, who did many of the gladiator films. Federico was short but super handsome, with dark skin and a rough beard. At eighteen or nineteen he lived in the coolest house right on the water and drove a yellow Jaguar XKE that he would let me borrow. Federico and I kind of became a pair; we would go to parties together, hang out together, and try to hook up with girls together. He was really determined to follow in his father's footsteps and direct and produce films.

His sister Raffaella was going out with a guy named Jean Pierre, whose father owned a restaurant in Cap Martin called Le Pirate. People would come in and run up bills of $20,000 or more. His father, who I knew simply as "the pirate," would come out dressed in costume. All the waiters and staff wore red bandanas and striped shirts. What they were famous for was this: the pirate would come out with a bottle of champagne, which he would charge you for whether you ordered it or not, and pour himself a glass and smash it on the concrete floor. I remember seeing guests sitting around a table of twelve, and suddenly the animal feeling would come over them and they all started smashing their glasses on the floor before even tasting the champagne.

Raffaella and I and my girlfriend at the time would go to the discotheque just down the street from Le Pirate, and then we'd show up about four in the morning ready for a free snack at the restaurant. I was amazed by the piles and piles of broken glasses and plates that the staff had swept up by that time. I asked Jean Pierre, "How does this work?" He said his father charges for each plate broken, and what's even cooler is he had this deal with a plate manufacturer somewhere near Nice to get all the seconds at a cut-rate price. I began to see that whatever happened in business, everybody had an angle. Even here, the seeming reckless abandon had an element of calculation.

Raffaella and Federico De Laurentiis were my first connection to the film business. Raffaella became a producer of a number of films, including *Dune*.

I was invited to lots of parties there in Monaco, sometimes due to the fact that I was the token hippie; nobody else in Monte

Carlo even had long hair. I think they wanted one of everybody at their parties. Overall, my look just attracted curious individuals.

At one point, I was sitting in the lobby of the Hotel de Paris when an older woman sat next to me and introduced herself as Tamara de Lempicka. She was wearing a big-tent-size floral dress and a big puffy artist hat, and we started a conversation that led to a really wonderful friendship. She was born in Poland and had become a famous Art Deco painter, with pieces displayed in some of the biggest museums all around the world. She also had mad love affairs with counts and dukes all across Europe. She was now in her seventies and living in the hotel but had recently been scammed by an art dealer who convinced her—through a partner who was a doctor—that she was about to die. Thinking she would soon be deceased, she sold off her personal art collection for hardly anything.

With that, she invited me up to her room in the hotel, where she had an easel and a painting that she was working on. While it was great to witness a brilliant artist and her craft, it was just devastating watching her trying to control the shaking of her hand as she tried to rebuild her personal collection of her own paintings.

However, she took a liking to me and introduced me to Andy Warhol, who was traveling through Monaco at the time along with his whole entourage: his business manager, Fred Hughes, and Bob Colacello, who was the editor and publisher of *Interview* magazine. We all hit it off and they asked me to travel around the south of France and through the Italian Riviera with them for the next three months as they raised money for a Puerto Rican musical. We would go from one wealthy person's house to the other.

Andy would do Marilyn Monroe–style portraits for each one and sell it for $25,000.

At the end of this trip, Andy gave me a signed Marilyn Monroe lithograph. Regrettably, a year or so later in the midst of an argument with my German girlfriend, I left the apartment and forgot the lithograph under my bed. I never saw it again. It just was one of those things that I continued to regret. On a regular basis, I would try to look for anybody selling a comparable piece of art and almost cry for how valuable my piece would have been. But eventually I realized that I was spending more time thinking about what I didn't get rather than being grateful for what I had.

I spent the next couple of years jumping from one project to another. First I was working for a former Italian general selling plastic mold–injected military insignias to countries in the Middle East. Then I was working for a guy named John Payne, who was selling investments in US start-ups.

John was tall and tan with slicked-back hair, and while he had no chewing gum in his mouth he always seemed to be chewing. He had a big Bob Hope grin and was always moving. He befriended me in the Café de Paris while I was just saying goodbye to a few of my Italian friends.

John worked for Investors Overseas Services (IOS), which was run by Bernie Cornfeld and the infamous Robert Vesco. Vesco, born in 1935, was an American financier who was once considered a boy wonder of international finance but later became a fugitive and died in 2007 in Havana. Vesco and Cornfeld were what they called wheeler-dealers, and John was an aspiring one. He noticed that I was friends with a number of wealthy Italians and offered me a sales job selling shares in private US companies, including one called Bionyx that made a tiny valve that was supposed to allow you to turn your vasectomy on or off at will. He taught me how to sell by focusing on what made the potential buyer tick and how an investment could meet their interests. He used role-playing to teach me to sell based on greed and fear. I was struck by how he tried to instill a fear of missing out on a golden opportunity. He had a huge impact on me—and I knew then that I would never want to be a salesperson.

I even tried to work a deal with a property developer trying to buy and develop the house I was living in, there in Monaco. The deal made perfect sense; everybody was going to get rich. But it never happened, because the owners of the house, an old couple, behaved irrationally about it. I began to see that it was not just business deals that made things work, but people, and people don't always do what makes economic sense. When I met the Nobel-winning economist Richard Thaler years later and heard his theory that consumers don't always act in their own interest, I finally had my explanation for why the couple wouldn't sell.

In late September 1973 a friend of mine, the photographer Claude Vaccarezza, and I decided to go for a photo adventure in Egypt. By that time, I had been to Cairo numerous times commissioning large canvas appliqué awnings for restaurants and had made friends with Nasr Salem, the son of the mayor of the Cairo suburb of Heliopolis. We decided to tour the desert south and east of Cairo in Nasr's Mercedes, taking pictures for the day.

Claude had a telephoto lens. On one occasion he spotted, along the horizon, clouds and clouds of dust and then we saw, rumbling along, dozens of military trucks all piled high with some sort of tubes. We couldn't figure out what they were but, before we knew it—and thank God before we took any pictures—we were surrounded by military police that just came out of nowhere. The officers surrounded us and grabbed all our cameras, put us in a Jeep, and took us to a nearby military base. We were all now in a panic just trying to stay calm, though I was hoping Nasr's politically connected father could help us. Then these guys started making motions like we were in deep trouble.

They told us to wait in an office under guard as they went to develop our film. They thought we were spies, even as Nasr tried to explain that we were just friends taking pictures of the desert.

They didn't believe us at first, but luckily the pictures were just scenic shots of Egypt.

Finding nothing incriminating on our cameras, they took Nasr away and we never saw him again. They took Claude and me to the Hilton hotel in the center of Cairo where we had been staying, walked us to our rooms, and made us shove all our possessions into our suitcases. Claude had also bought this eight-foot-tall brass hookah, and fortunately it came in two pieces, which he had bundled together with tape. With bags and bong in tow, they took us to the airport and sent us away on the very next flight out of Cairo.

We later learned that the trucks were carrying pontoon bridges heading toward the Suez Canal for the surprise attack led by Egypt and Syria on Israel for control of the Golan Heights and Sinai. Without knowing it, we had witnessed the start of the Yom Kippur War.

I had started this time period as a high school dropout on a quest for adventure and calculated reckless abandon. Somehow, along the way, I'd traveled all over Europe and met some of the most creative people in the world. I'd made, lost, and made mini-fortunes several times over. I felt different. I realized that despite all the books I'd read as a teenager, it was my experiences with people and finding business opportunities in between the reckless abandonment that had excited something inside me.

I spent two more years in Monte Carlo and in 1975, having received an amnesty from avoiding the draft, I thought it was time to go back to California and see if I could make something of myself.

TAKEAWAY

Life and the world around us is an amazing cauldron of people, places, history, trends, and ideas. It is impossible and in fact damaging to think you can plot your course in a planned, methodical way. The twists and turns and especially the unexpected is what makes life so exciting.

[3]

CAPTAIN VIDEO AND THE VIDEO DROID

Samma Kammanta (Right Action)
Our actions should be well meaning, constructive, and with
the highest sense of care and thoughtfulness for the world,
people, and family around us.

After I returned from Europe, I was ready to settle down and figure out something useful to do back home. I'd learned to look for new angles and new ideas, and to be curious, but I was about ready to figure out something that wouldn't require so much travel and risk.

I had shipped a dozen boxes home from Monaco all addressed to my mom, who lived with her fourth husband down a miles-long dirt driveway across the road from Muir Woods. Her husband, Roger, was a homebuilder and architect as well as a crazy saxophone player. Fifteen years earlier, along with two friends, he had purchased ten acres of the valley leading to Muir Beach for $10,000. It was a totally hip place with an open meadow between three houses and a huge woodworking shop. Often Roger would invite a dozen musicians he had randomly met, and soon a hundred or so guests would show up on a weekend to pound drums, make music, and get high.

My former girlfriend Juli had since married an English guy named Mick and we all decided to rent a house in Mill Valley together. We found a small two-bedroom cabin-style house and were moving in September 15. Since it would be more convenient, I thought I would stop by the new house on the 11th and ask the tenants that were moving out if I could store some boxes in their garage. When I got to the house and knocked on the door in my motorcycle jacket and mirror shades, a dark-haired petite Latina wearing super low-cut jeans answered the door. She was alone and clearly exhausted. I told her who I was and she asked me in. The place was covered in moving supplies: boxes, tape, scissors, packing material. She threw herself back on the couch. I could tell that her patience was wearing thin as I looked around. Then I asked her if I could leave my boxes in her garage tomorrow. Without hesitation she spat out, "Fuck no, I have enough shit to deal with!" Disappointed but not deterred, I switched subjects as I leaned on the counter and asked, "Well, how about we go to dinner tonight?" Surprisingly, she said yes. I returned later, we went to dinner, and I spent the night. In fact, she never moved out. I later learned that while her roommate had a new place, she had nowhere to go. That was Zamora. I married her and we spent the next forty-two years together.

For the next six years we continued the Germany-Hungary-Romania-Egypt runs, opened an art gallery in San Francisco, and made friends with a small group of like-minded world traveler importer-exporters who came from Bhutan, Europe, Indonesia, and elsewhere. We would put on shows with collectibles from exotic places and art shows of album cover painters for New Age and rock records. We did okay and lived in the back of our store on Washington Street in San Francisco. We had no car, just a moped. I learned the basics of cash flow in running a small business and how important it is to keep your vendors in the know, especially when, more often than not, we were unable to pay on time.

The business of video rentals had started in 1980, and it fascinated me. I had grown up as a latchkey kid watching television from the moment my brother and I would get home from school to the time my parents came home at six, expecting us to have our homework done. The idea that you could select what you want to watch on video, and then when to watch it, was a revelation. A small chain called Captain Video had four stores in the San Francisco Bay Area, one of very few video stores in the region.

I quickly became a totally fanatic customer. There was a $100 membership fee, rentals were $5 for a couple of nights, and the selection was pretty limited. I went to the one in San Anselmo, which was around eight hundred square feet, about the size of a small doctor's office. I was there almost every other day; I would typically rent two or three movies and buy two or three blank cassettes. I had two VCRs at home and I would just make copies of everything that I rented. My favorite titles were films like *Lawrence of Arabia* and, of course, all of Humphrey Bogart's films like *Casablanca* and *The Maltese Falcon*. Comedies as well, like *Fletch*. I wouldn't watch the shows again; what I really was looking for was total control: the ability to watch a movie whenever I wanted, wherever I wanted so long as I had a TV and a VCR. I had drawers and drawers of copies of movies in a kind of a chest that I had built to hold my TV.

One day, one of the four partners in Captain Video said to me, "Listen, you know we're looking to expand the business and we're wondering if you might want to loan us some money. We'll give you a high interest rate and we will give you free rentals and discounts on blank tapes." I had saved up around $20,000 from my work importing and exporting, and I thought, what a good deal. I'd get a high interest rate—which was something like 20 percent in the high-interest early '80s—and I'd probably save myself $100 a week just from the free rentals. So I loaned them the money.

I started getting really interested in the way they were running the business. At that time small businesses didn't use computers with point-of-sale systems—most computerized systems were in large companies. Here's how they kept track of things: They tracked each customer with a 3-by-5 card filled out with all their information and a membership number that was just sequential based on when you signed up. Each cassette had a unique label identifier on both the cassette itself and the case. Since credit cards were rare, every time you rented they would do a triplicate receipt with the name of the movie, your name, and your membership number. One copy of the receipt would go inside the cassette that you took home with you along with the date the movie was due to be returned, one copy was paper-clipped to that 3-by-5 membership card, and one went into the stack of daily receipts that would get totaled up at the end of the day.

To see if someone hadn't returned a movie on its due date, they would spend hours each day thumbing through shoeboxes filled with cards and they'd have to look at each one of them to know whether they should be calling somebody about the missing tape. If the customer came back without the receipt in the case, they'd have to look things up manually, flipping through every single card.

I realized, after I had loaned them the money, that I really didn't know much about the partners other than conversations that had happened when I was a customer. This was the first of many, many uninformed investments I made and, whether unfortunately or fortunately, continue to make.

A few months later, when I had just left the store, one of the partners came out and said, "Hey, you know, we don't think we can keep paying your interest." As I asked why, I noticed a white powder around his left nostril. In an edgy voice, he explained, in more detail than needed, all the things they spent the money on. I pointed out that the original loan was for store expansion, which they hadn't started on.

A couple of days later I came back and found the door locked. It took me a few days to get them on the phone, after which they told me they were closing and if I wanted a few movies in exchange for my $20,000 they would meet me at the store. I had been too trusting. I suppose I should have learned from that experience that you need to find out about the people you're working with, ideally prior to investing.

This was karma—but it turned out to be good for me in the end. I'd tried to help some people out, they'd cheated me but it also launched me onto a path that would define my career.

In the end I was able to round up five hundred movies from them and I left the store, stuffing them into my tiny green convertible Fiat Spider. What had driven a business doing half a million dollars in annual revenue into bankruptcy? "Internal theft"—stealing from the register—too many partners, not paying attention to cash flow by overbuying inventory? This was when it dawned on me that an automated movie rental kiosk could control both internal and even external theft.

In those days the video rental business was still forming and establishing rules and policies. The sellers of cassettes, both Beta and VHS format, were still unsure whether it was better to sell outright, license, or rent and do revenue sharing with the store. Unfortunately, most of those options would rely on accounting, and with the lack of computerized point-of-sale systems, there wasn't much to rely upon. So the studios and their distributors were each taking different approaches to the business.

My interest in the video business over the decades has revealed the same pattern repeated over and over again. Six studios have, more or less, dominated the movie business and TV business for many decades: Disney, Fox, Paramount, Sony, Universal, and Warner. These studios welcomed new revenue streams but were always fearful of any new distribution technology. They have a maniacal desire for control. They will attempt to torpedo or undermine any new tech that threatens that control. And because the consumer will do almost anything to increase convenience and control, the studios' attempts to beat back new technology almost always fail.

As you'll see in the rest of this book, I've been at the center of many of these shifts—always focused on what the consumer wants—and as a result, I've often found myself on the forefront of industry battles and at odds with the studios.

Videocassettes were one of the first battles in this long-running conflict. In 1976, Disney and Universal brought a suit known as the Betamax case, which claimed that Sony, a producer of VCRs (which also had a studio division), was damaging their profits with a device that could allow customers to record content without paying the holders of the copyrights to that content. Disney and Universal lost this case for good in 1984, when the Supreme Court ruled that VCRs were legal for consumers to record with.

Video rental was booming. It would generate $1.5 billion per year by 1985, double the revenues from the previous year. And if you added that to sales of rights to television broadcast, 1985 was also the first year that movies on TV sets generated about the same amount of revenue as movies at the box office.

The customer just wanted more and more and more. In those days you could succeed as a video rental store almost no matter what you did, provided you didn't open a store in the middle of nowhere. So many of us baby boomers absolutely loved movies and had resigned our mentalities to vegging out on unrewarding diversions from the real world, so the modest cost of a movie rental was the most affordable entertainment possible.

And with this newfound freedom from the strict TV schedule, we were all in. I can't stress enough the sense of liberation that came from not having to wait for Disney's Sunday 7:30 p.m. movie. Now you could watch what you wanted when you wanted. At the core of this newfound freedom was a ragtag group of movie lovers who mortgaged their homes, borrowed money from their moms, or scraped up money from their savings to open and run video rental stores.

Soon these stores became the place to be, much like the "general store" of the past, where you not only went to find a film for yourself but to hang out and talk films with fellow film lovers. Video stores tended to be an enjoyable place for many of us. Of course, we had our "crazies" as well—especially during the day when you had a mix of unemployed or retired men and mothers prepping for the evening's entertainment.

The backdrop for all of this was a fight over revenues. It was eye-opening to watch firsthand the friction between the incumbent major studios and the quickly growing cadre of indie and small-chain video rental stores. Both saw the potential for big dollars, but there was no agreement on how to divide the spoils. Neither side trusted the other.

Each side overvalued their contribution to the revenue path over the other's. The creative community that made the films undervalued the studios, while the studios undervalued the retailers—a dynamic that was carried over from theatrical movie distribution.

The precedent from other forms of movie distribution was murky. The studios had historically taken a percentage of revenue from movie theaters. But when they licensed to broadcast for cable television, they were always guaranteed a certain amount of money based on the viewership of that particular channel.

With video rental growing so fast, studios wanted their cut. For example, Warner devised physical and location-based audit systems to create different videocassette tapes for rental and for sale. I remember the first time I saw these big blue plastic "clamshell" cases that contained Warner rental movies sitting clumsily on the shelves of the Captain Video store. The idea was that the store would record each rental and pay Warner its share of the revenue.

This was my first encounter with how paranoia from studio executives resulted in what I felt was an overly complicated and unwieldly system. For the studio executives, it was as if the worst thing that could happen was rentals they didn't get a cut of. I saw that kind of paranoia create problems for consumers over and over in my career. On the other hand, knowing now how my partners had operated, I could not blame the Warner executives for their concern. After all, that's how I lost my $20,000. After getting to know many other video store operators, I found that there were plenty that had the same owner-operator mentality of finding every way to cut a dollar of cost whether it was honest or not.

Legally, though, the crux of the issue was a principle called the first-sale doctrine, established since 1908, which says that when you buy a copyrighted work, you can rent or sell or display it and make money however you want (except for making copies, of course). It's just like the way that Hertz or Avis can buy a Ford car and rent it to consumers and not pay Ford every time they rent it. Despite this principle, there were many attempts to control different formats of content. The studios did make an attempt through Congress to make movies an exception, as had previously been done for computer software and music, which you can't rent or exhibit without paying the copyright holder.

This was really the first time I learned that in launching a new way to sell or generate revenue from a product that had been around for a while, like movies, there would be this battle royale between the incumbent players and us innovators who were trying to improve the experience for the customer and perhaps create a new revenue stream. The incumbents were fighting mightily to preserve the stability of their existing revenue stream. Later I learned that this was really driven by individual interests, because every studio executive had goals and bonuses based on meeting or exceeding previous revenue and profit milestones.

With these new models, the predictability of that got all thrown up in the air. The trouble with new models, like video rental, is that they aren't just incremental; the studio executives thought if everybody goes to the video store they're going to go to the movie theaters less and they're going to watch television with commercials less. While the studios may make some money on the video stores, that will cannibalize the other channels and maybe even make the entire pie smaller. (Of course, as it turned out, all those channels vastly *increased* the total studio revenue.)

The clunkiness of video rentals made me start to think about the importance of simplicity. Was there a better way?

I took my five hundred videos, along with the last remains of the money I had saved up, and looked for a location, not to open a store in, but to learn about the business. My idea was to build a vending machine, a kiosk with a touchscreen monitor that would show trailers and information about the movies inside the kiosk. You would operate it by activating it with a credit card. You would pick your movies and the touchscreen would communicate with the vending machine and dispense the VHS cassette.

Of course, I knew nothing about design or computers or touchscreens or graphics or anything like that. So I went and bought my first computer so I could understand it. There was a store in San Rafael called Computer Time. Sean, a freckle-faced young sales guy who worked there, seemed to know a lot about computers. We really got along and after I bought the computer, I told him about my idea to create a computer-driven kiosk as a way to rent and even sell media like videocassettes.

He jumped on board with my idea. He had just started a young family with a wonderful supportive wife and two little kids.

We would meet every couple of days to brainstorm these ideas. We knew we needed designers, someone who could design the physical kiosk, and someone else to do graphics. We needed more sophisticated computer programmers, too.

One of the people living near my mom at the end of the dirt driveway was this designer named Kim Hicks, a handsome, slender, six-foot-four guy with a Beatle haircut. Kim was both a carpenter and a designer, and eventually he started working for movie companies building sets.

I asked Kim if he could design the kiosk and the appearance of the vending machine. He came back with some prototypes that were just fantastic. We then went out and found a guy named Dusty Parks who was a graphic designer, and we recruited a programmer, too. We formed a group that would design the programming for the kiosk to come up with the graphics and the touchscreen menu and kind of figure it all out.

Another creative friend of mine, Jerry, came up with some names for the thing. Our favorite was Video Droid, since after *Star Wars*, everyone knew a droid was a robot ready to help you out.

I invited my brother, Mark, to join us on the project. Mark was a doer; he always had a project to do whether it was to add a room to his house or help me find what was missing from my vending machine project. He recognized that the missing skill was mechanical engineering. He identified an electrical engineering company called Essex Engineering in Connecticut who told us that they could build the machine that would dispense the tapes, for $10,000. We decided that Mark should move out there and live in the nearby area to be able to manage and check up on them.

Little did we know that they were going to come back with a converted candy sales machine with simple solenoid switches. When you press, say, A6, it would turn a little hook that would let the item fall from a rack into a bin below, where you could then pull it out. As you may remember, those old candy machines were quite heavy and big: six or seven feet tall, four or five feet wide, and two or three feet deep. With Mark's supervision and management we eventually got the first one shipped to San Francisco.

Having seen all the internal theft, lack of control, and high costs of opening and operating a video store, I really thought that the Video Droid machine was the best idea ever. I was sure this was a perfect solution, since you could put them anywhere, from the front of grocery stores where people shop, to hotels and hospitals where people are stuck for a long period of time.

The machine included a credit card reader, would print out a receipt, and would wire the charges and deposit them into my account. We hadn't automated a way to take the cassette back and make it available for the next customer; instead, there was a little sliding drawer you could use to return it. When you slid the drawer back in, a barcode reader would identify it and decide whether it needed to charge the customer's account more. It also required a worker to come by on a regular basis, restock the VHS cassettes, and bring in new inventory.

I looked for an office we could use to gather the team and start building these kiosks and displays and launching the technology and sales teams. Like many first-time entrepreneurs, I had grandiose plans without any experience starting a business. I learned very quickly that things were never going to work the way that I had expected them to.

I found a location for the company that, coincidentally, was not only 3,200 square feet of inexpensive office space but could also double as a great retail location with eight parking spaces out front. I started with the five hundred movies I'd gotten from Captain Video. I thought we could build a small enclosure out front for the video rental store and do our development work building the touchscreen and the kiosk in back.

I ended up also using Kim Hicks to design the interior of the store. I thought, why should we look like every other video store with flat walls and racks? So we built a curvy set of walls that undulated back and forth with custom shelves, spray-painted with graphics of planets and blue and purple highlights. We opened the store with the five hundred cassettes, and we went out and bought a couple of cardboard file boxes and a stack of 3-by-5 cards so we could use the same triplicate receipt method that they'd used at Captain Video, at least until we got the vending machine we were building in the back working.

The machine was coming together, featuring a picture of Danny Droid, which was our robotic video store clerk who had an encyclopedic knowledge of movies and the inventory available to rent. Danny Droid's face was on the touchscreen, with a funny little oval-shaped head. When I say *touchscreen*, you need to understand that these were not the touchscreens you are familiar with now, like the one on an iPhone. These used a grid of invisible infrared lights on all sides of the screen; when you touched the screen the grid detected where your finger was and used that to manage the dispensing of the cassettes. I believe we were one of the very first kiosk companies that built a touchscreen and built it into a point-of-sale device.

Based on my broad and varied experiences in Europe, I did know one thing: that you need to seek help and advice wherever you can. I knew that we were going to have to understand the video rental business a lot more deeply than I did just from my customer visits and ill-fated investment in Captain Video. The Video Software Dealers Association (VSDA) had just been established in 1981 and was setting up chapters around the country. I thought, this is the perfect way to meet other experienced people in the business in a noncompetitive setting. They had their first meeting over in Alameda mostly because Ken Dorrance, one of the guys who organized the group, ran a store called Video Station in Alameda.

He had been in the business since its very beginning. He was a big teddy bear kind of guy with bright red hair and freckles, always in a good mood. His wife, Peggy, was very brainy and complemented Ken's more adventurous personality.

This being a nascent regional organization, they were looking for volunteers to be on their board of directors. I thought, what a perfect way for me to get close to the smartest and most experienced people, so I volunteered and was elected and then appointed vice president of the regional association. That began fifteen years or so of my being involved in the trade association and learning from and interacting with other smart people in the industry.

As we went further on developing the kiosk vending machine idea, I realized that I needed a more experienced group of developers and technical people, including manufacturers and salespeople. A friend of mine in Japan introduced me to the folks at OMRON, one of the biggest ATM manufacturers in the world. I realized they were dispensing bills based on a menu screen with instructions and push buttons, which I thought would make them a perfect partner. I went to Japan with Jim McCarthy, a partner of mine in Video Droid. After we met with them and their partners from another company, C. Itoh, for a few days, they said, "We will take all your ideas and create a prototype machine that is more sophisticated than the candy machine prototype that you have." The big ask was to develop a machine that would automatically restock the VHS cassettes when they were returned, so it could continue renting movies between the visits of a service employee to restock inventory.

These meetings to explore the product design and the business opportunity were incredibly revealing and educational. They asked all the right questions for anyone starting or investing in a business: Who is the customer? How are you going to acquire customers? What does the customer want? What is the pricing and how does it compare to the competition? What's the cost of operation? How are you going to secure locations? Since I had not been to business school or previously operated a business, this opened my eyes to how difficult and complicated it was. Yes, you can have a passionate desire to launch a business around your clever idea, but there was so much more to it. As seemed to happen so often in my career, I was hip deep in something before I got the chance to learn how it really worked.

In making these deals, I learned that people you are trying to do deals with rarely tell you what they have in mind. Meanwhile, people like me have this vision of a big deal, a way to become rich. I mentally went off in some crazy fantasy world where relationships with C. Itoh would pan out—but they had nothing like that in mind; they were just trying to learn as much as they could from me, a punk kid with an idea. I eventually learned that putting together a project like this, including design, manufacturing, distribution, and operations, is incredibly complicated, because it takes lots of people headed in the same direction who are prepared to commit.

I also learned about synchronization and how important it is in any business deal. If one group is way ahead of the other, or investing time and money, while the other sees the deal developing in two or three years, you are not going to succeed. It's also about intentions, trying to understand other people and other companies' intentions. In this deal, I was going fast, and C. Itoh and its people were going super slow.

As things weren't going so well, I felt betrayed by those big Japanese companies; I felt like I was being led on. But I learned a lesson, which was not blaming other people. When I started blaming them, I realized I was being stupid. It was me not understanding that they had completely different intentions. I was blind to seeing what they were saying. They weren't dishonest. All I had to do was ask, but I never asked. You always have to put the responsibility on yourself, be thoughtful and organized, and not be afraid to ask, "What do you really want here?"

Eventually, after about a year and a half we had a handsome prototype machine about the size of a small Coca-Cola machine with a beautiful white plastic façade, featuring backlit box covers with buttons to designate the movies you might want to rent. There was also a touchscreen monitor where you could see previews and more information about the film. The inside of the machine was incredibly complex but efficient. When a cassette was returned, the machine identified it from a barcode, logged it as returned on the customer's account, and put it in the right bin. The buttons for the films would light up when the film was available and stay dark when it was out of stock.

At that point I started going around to grocery stores, hotels, hospitals, and other types of locations. But everyone I met with said the same thing: "Why would I want to put a machine here when there's literally a video store opening up around almost every corner?" (This was before Blockbuster or Hollywood Video, but independent stores were opening at a very fast rate; by that time there were about twenty thousand independent locations around the country, twice as many locations as McDonald's.) The general perception was there didn't need to be more locations to be able to rent cassettes. On top of that, consumers weren't comfortable with the credit card usage and the necessary deposit for the tape. Plus, they were worried about who was going to be storing their data.

After hitting my head against the wall for about six months, I finally decided to call it a day. That was depressing, but in the end I learned a huge amount from the experience.

Shutting down the vending machine project wasn't that hard a decision, because while all this was going on, the video store, also called Video Droid, was growing every single day. We had so many customers we ended up having to push the walls back. Finally, we decided to take back the remaining square feet we were reserving for the work on the kiosk and expand the store.

I had set out to revolutionize the movie rental industry with an amazing machine. I'd had that machine built. And I'd failed to turn it into a business, even as I backed into running a very successful video store.

Now I dedicated myself to becoming a good small business owner running my single 3,200-square-foot video rental store. I needed to learn the basics and then the strategies of running a store: location, employees, inventory planning, promotion and marketing, products and services, pricing and forecasting. Forecasting I found to be a much bigger subject than cash flow or profit, since it was your guide to where you wanted to take your business, how you would get there, and how you would measure up to milestones. You had to model how much product or service margin was needed, what was your fixed overhead, what was your competition doing, and where were the consumer trends going. I became immersed in reading everything about retail and movies and talking to other business leaders, others in this new video rental business, and most of all, our customers. For the next thirteen years I spent roughly twenty-five thousand hours on my stores, thirteen thousand of which were on the floor talking or transacting with customers.

I joined the local chamber of commerce. I chaired the local Memorial Day parades. I volunteered to be on the county planning commission, I joined other trade associations, and I participated in numerous other local, regional, and national projects.

I also decided to dedicate myself to my family in a way my own father never had—which would be easy since he left when I was eight years old. I swore that I would stay put for my three kids' schooling years. We lived in about the best place you could imagine, Mill Valley, California, full of beautiful nature, just across the Golden Gate Bridge from San Francisco, wealthy, healthy, and surrounded by highly educated high-performance professionals, great public and private schools, and lots of opportunities for extracurricular activities for kids. I jumped in with huge enthusiasm.

I coached my oldest son Joaquin's Little League teams and was his Cub Scout pack den leader, coached and assistant-coached my daughter Paloma's fast-pitch softball team, and assistant-coached my youngest son Emiliano's Little League teams. On top of that, I attended thirty or forty games a year among all the kids, often racing back and forth from one field to another to catch part of each child's games when there was a conflict. But there was a lot I failed at. Rarely if ever did we all sit down at the table and eat together, discuss serious life issues, or travel together.

I was prouder of Joaquin, Paloma, and Emiliano than anything I had ever done in my life. They meant the world to me. They educated me more than I did them, and they kept me sane and rational. And my wife, Zamora—who, like me, had had a difficult childhood—was beautiful, caring, loving, and an amazing mother. She was also a huge supporter of mine and made sure that everything was safe and perfect for the kids, with lots of ideas for things they could do to enrich themselves.

All this positive activity was like a deposit in the karmic bank for me. I have so much luck, sometimes it seems as if an angel is protecting me. I go back to the things that I think are good and selfless—and this was the period in which I started to understand how important that was.

My ability to succeed at business was part of this grounded life. I got pretty good at it. I was detail-oriented, thoughtful, frugal when needed, and willing to invest when the opportunity showed itself.

My brother, Mark, became my partner and my most valuable leader. For the next thirty years, Mark was the operational leader of that first store and eventually a whole chain of stores in Marin and

Sonoma Counties just north of San Francisco. His operational excellence gave me the time to focus on identifying a profitable cost structure, budgeting for new inventory, managing employees, and investing in fixed costs and advertising.

We were known as the eclectic video store in our market. Whereas the typical video store carried five thousand titles and focused on lots of copies of the big hits, we would carry twenty thousand to thirty thousand titles. We were one of the first to carry complete seasons of TV shows you could get from free TV. Our silent section was four rows high and five feet wide, and our foreign and documentary sections were the best in the country. And in those days, like almost all other rental outlets, we carried porn.

This section was cordoned off with curtains hiding the often lewd box covers. Our porn customers were typically older men, probably single and a bit sleazy, but the profits were better than any other product we carried. We would pay between $5 and $20 for a VHS cassette and rent it for $3 about fifty times, then sell it used for $5. We worked with a Playboy Enterprises distributor and would even have in-person autographing appearances of Playmates of the Month, which for some reason seemed to attract every law enforcement officer in the area.

Being in the wealthier areas outside San Francisco, we also had our fair share of celebrity customers. One afternoon while I was ringing up a video rental I received a call from the police in Sausalito, which was the next town over from Mill Valley. The officer identified himself and then asked to speak to the owner. He asked me to come over to their office and identify some recovered stolen merchandise that included a number of VHS cassettes from our store.

When my shift ended at five p.m., I drove to the police station and was taken back to an inventory room. There was a large cardboard box with about ten VHS cassettes covered in white powder—which I was worried was drugs, but turned out to be fingerprint powder. The titles covered the range from soft porn to kinky. Most of the softer porn titles had our store stickers on them. I asked the officer where they were found.

He asked me if I knew Hunter S. Thompson, which of course I did. For around six months he had been spending a half hour daily in the porn section talking to himself and leaving with an armful of movies. The officer told me that Mr. Thompson's house in Sausalito had been robbed and these tapes were recovered from the robbery.

He was hardly our only celebrity customer. Our other customers included the Grateful Dead, Peter Coyote, Robert Culp, and many writers and directors. George Lucas and people working at his studio Skywalker Ranch were also customers. I learned that the hard way: by receiving a cease-and-desist demand from George Lucas's lawyers demanding that we change our name, taking the Droid out of Video Droid.

This was one of my first experiences with legal issues, and the lessons I learned about how to deal with "the big boys" helped me many times, though not always successfully. At this time, Lucas had several products using the Droid name, not to mention the characters from Star Wars. He had the Droids and Ewoks cartoon shows and a system called the EditDroid, which was a new way to edit movies. He obviously thought that our use of Droid was an infringement.

Little did he or his lawyers know, but I had trademarked Video Droid a few years before he had. My lawyer Beverly Green sent him a kind letter passing on our previous trademark info. Soon after we received a similarly kind letter stating that they were prepared to fight my trademark. Now it wasn't as if I was going to lose my business, but by that time I had spent a lot on signage and, more importantly, on our brand. We were known as the Droid, as in "Hey, let's go rent some movies at the Droid."

I found myself internally exaggerating the impact and cost of this and, with little experience in bargaining, asked Beverly for advice. She suggested that we propose keeping the name, but only for use on rental stores, and letting Lucas get the Droid trademark on everything else. Lucas's lawyer agreed, and Skywalker Ranch became a good-sized long-term customer. Beverly recently told me that Lucas's lawyer has the letter from her framed in his office as a great example of working things out. I was relieved and learned a good lesson: not to overreact.

Over the years my brother and I added a bunch of new services and new business to our core rental stores. The first thing we did was to add locations. We considered franchising but rejected it, which was probably a mistake. Two of our customers, Winsor and Sam Orrick, wanted to get into the business, so we created two partnerships, one for a second store in Mill Valley and the other for our third store in San Rafael. The San Rafael store was in a big space that was formerly a car dealership showroom. The huge space inspired us to create a series of movie sets, including a two-story-high wall with a likeness of Indiana Jones scaling the wall and trying to reach a treasured object in a recess near the top. Customers entered another room along a yellow brick road, and the room was decorated with the witch's castle and the flying monkeys from *The Wizard of Oz*.

The sets we built were so successful that we started a subsidiary called Chameleon Productions, which built sets for other retailers as well as in-store merchandising commissioned by major studios such as Paramount. To promote *The Hunt for Red October* for Salzer's Video in Ventura, California, we built the nose of a gigantic submarine jutting out from the exterior wall of the freestanding store. Once we had remade the outside of his store on a high-traffic street in Southern California, the owner got unintentional added exposure; the nose of the submarine was a little too long and thin not to conjure up images of a man's genitals. Well, you know what they say, all publicity is good publicity.

I learned a lot from other more practiced video store owners, some of whom had built pretty significant businesses. By this time, we had opened another two stores and purchased five more, bringing our chain up to a total of ten stores generating $3 million to $4 million in annual revenues. As I got more and more active in the leadership of the VSDA, I found that our members' stores were getting attacked from many sides. There were around two hundred proposed state and federal laws that would either tax our industry or regulate how we displayed product. I joined the legislative team at VSDA. When speaking to state legislators and members of Congress, I realized that they thought of us as porn dealers and not legitimate hardworking businesspeople.

Around that time in 1989, a movement called Rock the Vote, originated by the music industry, was gathering steam. The objective was to get young people to register to vote. NARM, a sister organization of VSDA that also served retailers, had spearheaded the drive. I proposed to the leaders of NARM and VSDA that we start a voter registration and registration education program in video stores.

We launched a pilot program in California for the 1990 election, and that did so well we decided to go national for 1992. We filmed four great public service announcements, which many studios inserted at the beginning of hundreds of thousands of VHS movies; thousands of video stores put up display materials on their counters, and in states where you could register by mail, like California, they handed out registration forms. Nationwide, we believe that we registered over five hundred thousand new voters for the 1992 elections. Since that election, politicians took our industry and our members much more seriously. I believe you should approach a weakness in your position by addressing that weakness instead of going after the other side; in this case, we realized a very efficient way to bring clout to our industry.

Despite working closely with Blockbuster in our Rock the Vote campaign, I was regularly terrified that they would decide to finally enter my area. I competed against small operators and our market share locally was around 50 percent. When we acquired one of those small chains it came with a wonderful location in the scenic town of Tiburon, California. The rent was reasonable, the location was large, and the display windows were all you could dream of. While I really wanted to do this expansion right, I was learning that by expanding beyond the number of locations that I or my brother or my partners could work at regularly, it was hard to maintain the customer-focused culture that small businesses are often known for.

When you are an owner-operator you are there working one-on-one with customers and staff. It is hardwired that without caring for your customers you could get wiped out by a big-box retail competitor in the snap of a second. But I had not yet learned how you design and manage team culture to replicate what the best of us owner-operators lived and breathed. I did know that I needed a customer-centric manager for the new store. I had always been impressed by the attitude and care my distributor rep showed us and thought she would make an ideal store manager.

After some incentives and coaxing, she agreed to move up from Los Angeles and take over. The store was starting to do really well and revenue was going up every month. Then one day I found that the store had not opened for the day at ten a.m. as usual. I learned that a Blockbuster had suddenly opened and hired away my manager along with a few other of my store employees. This was the first time I realized that you had to play hardball in business.

Because of the success of my voter registration campaign and another campaign I led that significantly reduced the worker's compensation fees video retailers paid, I was elected to the national board of directors of VSDA. Two years later in 1995 I became the manager of its national convention. I was slated to give the opening and welcoming speech to about three thousand attendees, but I had never given a speech before. I will never forget how terrified I was until my son Joaquin gave me a *Far Side* cartoon and said, "Just look at it before you go on stage."

The scene is a log cabin high on a hill. A man is sitting on the cabin's porch with a shotgun on his lap and his wife is sitting next to him. Below in the valley, arrayed in battle formation, are tanks, machine guns, and armed men all labeled *FBI*. The man with the shotgun has just turned to his wife and said, "I didn't think they took that FBI warning at the beginning of the video cassette so seriously."

The laugh that the cartoon brought helped me overcome my fear, and I think of it every time I speak in public.

One of the most beneficial aspects of serving on the VSDA board was that I had access to in-depth industry analysis and forecasting, just as the leaders of Hollywood Video or Blockbuster did. But I also had something they didn't, and I believe that this is the core to success. I continued to have hours and hours of first-hand customer interaction, which put a face on the data. This understanding of the customers and their needs, combined with the behind-the-scenes analytics, made for a deep understanding of the behavior of the evolving entertainment customer. I will always look back at this as my most important time of learning.

I had learned so much. I had surrounded myself with educated and successful people in the VSDA, and without the benefit of formal schooling, I was like a sponge, picking up on how they talked, what they knew, and where they learned it from. I learned the language of Harvard-educated people and presidents of multimillion-dollar companies—and I learned not only to know what I was talking about, but to *sound* like I knew. This was about to become very useful in the next stage of my career.

I had tasted failure in the creation of a video vending machine and success in the video rental industry. But I was not complacent, and my desire to innovate had not abated. And that was a good thing, because the opportunity to remake the video business was about to knock on my door.

───────────────── **TAKEAWAY** ─────────────────

Learning how to evaluate the integrity and intentions of people you want to work with can save you much pain and misery, not to mention money. What is really hard is balancing that with enthusiasm for the ambiguous and unknown. That is what makes life and business challenging: learning how to do both.

[4]

THE BIRTH OF NETFLIX

Samma Samadhi (Right Concentration)
We must focus on solving big challenges and answering the
most complex questions in life in business or in family.

Despite the false start with the videocassette vending machine, I found myself well suited to running a business, especially one so connected to my love of movies. I threw myself into the work. By late 1996, I'd been running video stores for twelve years, with my ten stores up and down California's Highway 101 stretching from Mill Valley to Santa Rosa. I had become friends with many of Video Droid's countless avid fans. We were a place for film lovers and aficionados of all kinds: families, singles, and even people in the film and TV business and those who saw themselves as amateur experts in the entertainment industry.

As I mentioned in the last chapter, our customers included many entertainment celebrities. Spending time on the floor of the video store talking movies with customers, local businesspeople, and the occasional film distributor rep gave me a chance to get to know about many diverse opinions, views, and perspectives on life, business, entertainment, love, and politics. We became kind of like the general store, a meeting place where just about everyone felt comfortable.

We were trying to innovate by building interesting Hollywood displays as well as merchandising a huge variety of theatrical-sized candies and treats, selling pizzas, duplicating people's home films, and even renting out 3D attachments and movies for your VCR. Each couple of months my brother, Mark, and I would explore some new ancillary business or revenue stream. It was logical since we all knew that someday stores would not be at the center of home entertainment distribution and we needed to identify the long-term business opportunities.

In hindsight, we were not really looking as far out-of-the-box as we should have been. We were putting Band-Aids on a dying business instead of building an entirely new one. Even though our business was generating hundreds of thousands of dollars a year in free cash flow, to me, it was clear that the end was near.

I was beginning to develop a more sophisticated view of myself and the world, mostly because of what I learned from the people I met. There were people like David Kalish, a cofounder of the software company Autodesk, who helped me to see a lot more about how technology and software worked in the context of a business and how to raise money, for example. And I'd acquired enough influence based on my local efforts with the VSDA to be chosen as its president. I felt like a student, learning from the masters all around me how to behave as a businessperson.

David Kalish introduced me to a friend named Eric Lyons. Eric was a software engineer who had had many successes. In 1995 David, Eric, and I agreed that video stores were well positioned to add an internet component. The video stores had thousands of titles to choose from, each with a synopsis and metadata like stars and directors to browse through. We added more titles weekly and customers had a voracious appetite for more information in their desire to make a good decision on what movie to bring home to the family. At this point, retail use of the internet as a storefront was new. Google's search engine had only just launched and Amazon was still advertising on the radio. But in the mid-nineties the mantra was to "build an internet presence" no matter how stupid or illogical your product was.

We conceived a menu-driven application for video stores to use to launch their own customized store website. In the late nineties there were around twenty thousand video stores around the country. Three chains had more than a thousand locations each, but there were fifteen thousand or more independent owners with only a few locations each. The service we launched would provide simple menu-driven tools for an indie owner to add their logo, location, and pricing info and to customize the inventory offering from an all-inclusive master list. They could also send out a newsletter and even sell used movies. Our idea was that a video store could sign up with our company called Nervous Systems Inc. (NSI), and for $25 per month per location you would join the internet revolution. In addition we would earn a percentage of sales and introduce new services over time.

Our big launch of NSI (I was a little embarrassed saying the full name of the company) occurred at the July 1997 VSDA convention in Las Vegas. The VSDA convention attracted video store owners as well as anyone who sold to them, including movie studios, distributors, point-of-sale systems, and interior display companies.

It was a big show, three hundred thousand square feet of exhibition space that ranged from spectacular ten-thousand-square-foot spaces for the movie studios down to ten-by-ten spaces for smaller suppliers like NSI. The exhibition brought in tens of millions of dollars for our trade association and we sold full passes to about four thousand attendees for $350 apiece. All the entertainment and meals were supplied by various studios and they would bring in big names like Ray Charles, Randy Travis, Leslie Nielsen, *Star Trek*'s James Doohan ("Scotty"), Steve Allen, Mike Myers, 49ers quarterback Steve Young, Orioles Hall of Famer Brooks Robinson, John Travolta, and Lucy Lawless ("Xena: Warrior Princess"). We had an award show where we would present celebrity awards, such as Celebrity of the Year or a Lifetime Achievement Award.

By the time of that show, NSI had sold subscriptions to around two hundred video stores, and we were trying to figure out how we could increase the price to make it profitable. The challenge was not delivering the service for each incremental subscription but rather covering our own salaries and a few small fixed costs. Even if we got to 20 percent of the small-operator locations, which would represent enormous growth, our revenue would just barely be sufficient to deliver a high-quality service. Despite the whole world "moving to the net," most indie video store operators were penny pinchers and could not look further into the future than next month's video releases. But armed with the exuberance of start-up founders believing that there was no way we couldn't succeed, we set ourselves up in that little booth at the convention.

I was doing triple duty. As president of VSDA, I had to give speeches, greet celebrities, and attend events. I also had the managers of my ten video stores looking at new products and ideas. Plus

I was working the booth to demo our new product. I felt like the Flash, racing from one event to the next. My wife and kids were there as well. It was pretty much the first time they had joined me and it was only because I thought they would be impressed by the gigantic suite that was comped for me at the Hilton hotel as president of the association. In the past, I'd come back from the convention with half a dozen movie logo giveaway T-shirts, coffee mugs, some theatrical candy, and other tchotchkes that I thought were cool but generated a lot of behind-my-back "Oh God, not another stupid shirt" remarks from my family. This time it would be different, I told myself. My partner in the video stores—my brother, Mark—brought his wife, Lynne, as well to keep Zamora entertained.

DVD, the new movie format introduced just a few months earlier, was a big focus at the convention. It was backed by the studios because it was cheaper to produce and distribute than the clumsily large VHS cassettes, with at least twice the picture and sound quality. There was no consensus from the studios or video rental chains yet on pricing, title selection, timing, and sell-through for the DVD format.

The home video executive at Warner Bros., Warren Lieberfarb, saw DVD as a huge boon to building a profitable business where millions of consumers would purchase libraries of their favorite movies and documentaries. Lieberfarb had his detractors. After all, LaserDiscs had many of the same characteristics as the flashy DVDs. But as Lieberfarb and others including me liked to point out, LaserDiscs were the size of LPs and not all were priced for retail, but more for high-end collectors. Some store owners were concerned that in the transition period they would be forced to take on the burden of carrying both VHS and DVD formats of the same movies, adding significant costs amid the uncertainty of the adoption rate of the new DVD players. In 1997, DVD players were still mostly selling at a price above $500.

At that time 80 or 90 percent of the video retail business was rentals, with just a few titles for sale at under $40 retail, including Disney classics and other films rereleased at a sell-through price after a year of rental. The wholesale price of most VHS movies was $70 to $90 per cassette. At that price, only video stores would buy them, and then rent them out forty to sixty times at $3 per rental.

Some studio leaders like Lieberfarb believed (accurately, as it turned out) that if we reduced the retail cost to $20, the studios would sell billions of dollars of DVDs. Other studios thought that those low prices would simply lower the cost of goods to video stores, and sales to consumers would not offset those losses. In 1997 the total annual rental revenue to studios was around $10 billion. Amid this uncertainty, there were many opinions and perspectives on the pros and cons of DVD, how to price it, how to launch it, and so on.

At the time there were only thirty or forty titles available on DVD, and they were not yet movies but nature and travel programs. The other complication with DVD in those early days was standardization. As a result, you might have a disk work in a Mitsubishi player but not a Pioneer player.

A few months before the event, as president of the association, I had established a DVD packaging committee that had representatives from both studios and retailers. The goal was to come up with packaging that would work for selling or renting DVDs, packaging that would be distinct from both VHS and music CDs but still fit on all of our shelving. The committee had reached a consensus that the height of the box that contained the DVDs would be the same across all studios, the same height as a VHS cassette and the same width as a music CD. The cases would be made of hard plastic with a clear sleeve over that so that the studio could slide in artwork on the front and the synopsis and other data on the back.

But as always happens with studios, their resistance to innovation and change caused problems.

One studio, Sony Pictures, decided to stick with the CD-type jewel case. That ended up being a disaster for rental stores since the weak plastic hinge would break after the first rental. At the convention, I ran into the president of Sony Home Video, Ben Feingold, at the entrance to a dinner event. I asked why he chose to not go along with the standards created by the joint committee. He had decided to save on the costs of tooling for new packaging, rather than create a package that distinguished itself from other formats and was durable enough for rentals. I suspected that he saw the less durable packaging as a way to drive consumers to purchase movies instead of renting them. I can't now recall exactly what he said, but I am sure it made sense from his perspective. Of course, within a few months, once Sony saw the disastrous customer complaints, they joined the other studios by releasing DVDs in the agreed-upon packaging.

As you'll read later in the book, this wasn't the last time that Ben and I ended up at odds.

The introduction of DVDs also initiated an interesting development that completely changed the course of my career.

One day at the convention, while I was in the NSI booth, a rugged, handsome guy carrying a small backpack and wearing running shoes came by. He started asking all these questions about the new DVD format, what I thought about rental pricing, viability, would it replace VHS, et cetera. As president of the trade association and a store operator, I was full of ideas and opinions, which I shared with him, more than once gently letting him know that most of his ideas had been tried or would not work. In hindsight I see that I should have understood that just because something did not work in the past was not a good forecast of the future. Then I glanced at what he was holding in his hand, which was our convention catalog folded open, showing my head shot on the front page.

At that point I became sure he was not a video store owner, hence not a potential customer for our internet service. He moved on to an unusual set of questions, like, "Would a DVD break if you bent it?" He wanted to know what sorts of things retailers were doing with mail order or home delivery. I shared with him that my brother had been an advisor to a home delivery company called Rabbit Video. They would install a special mailbox on the customer's front door. When the customer ordered a VHS title from a catalog the size of a big telephone book, it would be delivered to the mailbox later in the day. When they were finished with the movie, they would call the store and put the movie in the mailbox, and someone would come and pick it up. You would get charged on your credit card and order and return whenever you wanted to.

Now I am a very open, maybe a bit naïve, person when it comes to discussing topics and issues that interest me. In hindsight I probably sounded like a gushing kid going from one thought to another. It wasn't that my entire focus was on impressing this obviously smarter and more educated person than I was, but I'm sure that was part of it. More significantly, I saw that this guy was clearly a big step more aware of the world and especially more knowledgeable about business than I was, and I craved an opportunity to work with people like him. I had been spending a lot of time with indie video store operators, who are not a very sophisticated lot.

We went back and forth for about thirty minutes and then suddenly this guy said, "Okay, thanks, see ya."

Wait a minute, I thought. I don't even know your name. As he was walking away, I grabbed his backpack just below his neck and pulled him awkwardly and aggressively backward. I asked him, "So what's your name?" "Marc Randolph," he replied. Sensing that he needed to be a bit more polite, he gave me his contact info and said very loosely, and in hindsight I realize not sincerely, "Let's talk again."

That conversation turned out to be more important than anything else that happened at that conference.

A few weeks later I realized Marc hadn't followed up, so I gave him a call. (This was back before mobile phones, so I was calling his office, of course.) I am not sure if it was the second or third try, but eventually Marc answered. I reminded him of who I was and we agreed to meet around halfway between my place, in Mill Valley just north of the Golden Gate Bridge, and his Silicon Valley home near Santa Cruz.

At the time, Marc was the vice president of corporate development at a company called Pure Atria, where Reed Hastings was the president and the major shareholder. By 1997, a larger software company called Rational Software had reached terms to acquire Pure Atria and gave most of the employees severance through September. This left Marc and a few others with some valuable time to plot out their next career move.

We met the following week for lunch at Buck's Café in Woodside. Buck's was the place where Jeff Yang came up with Yahoo!, and many a vision for a start-up had been formulated on Buck's napkins. I remember feeling in awe of how smart Marc was as he described the details of his idea: a DVD retailer, operating exclusively online, that would rent and sell DVDs to consumers all over the country and mail them in a thin envelope, light enough for cheap first-class postage, which at the time was just thirty-two cents. The business would benefit from one centralized inventory serving the entire country, which meant you could include even the most esoteric long tail titles in your inventory. You would never have to worry about getting in your car to pick up or return the movies. And you could shop and browse online even in your underwear. Prices would be roughly the same as going to Blockbuster, which at the time was doing around one-third of all rental revenue.

I was incredibly impressed with Marc. Having never attended university myself, I was always fascinated by super smart, highly educated people. All my life I had been a voracious reader and traveler, so I knew a lot and could hold my own in a conversation with people like him, but I was like a sponge ready to absorb data and understanding from people more educated than I was. Marc was definitely one of those people. I had never heard someone talk about marketing and product fit and the kind of understanding of consumer behavior that Marc would share with me.

Marc was trying to get to know me better, including family, interests, education, and, more importantly, my movie rental experience. I felt like we hit it off well and Marc seemed to like my openness and my humility. Marc continued to keep his cards close to his vest and I found myself asking more and more questions about what he was up to. We agreed to meet the following week as well, toward the end of August in 1997.

In the days before we met, I was feeling the excitement and exhilaration of interviewing for the best job of my life.

First, we talked about my own innovations. I shared with Marc how I was always tinkering with new concepts and products/ services with our stores, including home delivery, and how my brother and I were doing work for several studios building massive store displays, like the submarine promoting *The Hunt for Red October* protruding from the building for Salzer's Video. He knew I was deeply involved in my trade association, which had on its board of directors the presidents of Blockbuster and Hollywood Video, so I felt like he respected my opinion on his questions. He was also impressed with our video store online subscription service. But looking at all of our hoped-for innovations, it didn't matter whether it was making copies of customers' home videos, renting 3D equipment, our subscription service, or VCR repairs: Marc found flaws in all these concepts. He was never shy about expressing them. While at first I was a bit sensitive, I learned over time that Marc's mind worked that way. In all the years since I have known Marc, I continue to be impressed by the way he can cut to the core of an idea and explore its flaws and then rebuild it better.

In this meeting, he began to describe the business concept in as much detail as he could, which still wasn't a lot for such an embryonic concept. It started with the concept of taking the

DVD out of its case and creating an envelope in which you could mail the DVD to anywhere in the United States with a first-class stamp. He already had conceived of designing the envelope so that it could be mailed back as well for the return. There was no concept at the time of a subscription, or the request queue, or recommendations, or original content, or any of the things that became part of what would be Netflix. The idea was simpler: a video store where you ordered online, received and returned DVDs by United States Postal Service (USPS) mail, and bought DVDs at a price point competitive with retailers like Walmart and Best Buy. He had two big gating questions:

1. Do you think rental customers will rent online and wait for home delivery?
2. Do you think the DVDs will break in the mail?

My not-very-well-considered answers to his questions were "Absolutely movie rental customers will rent online" and "Yes, the DVDs will be fine in the mail." This was despite the fact that my brother's and my experience with mail order was not positive and I really had no idea what would happen to a DVD in the mail. At the time neither Marc nor I knew that the USPS ran all first-class mail around steel rollers about eight inches in diameter, forcing anything inside the envelope to bend around the roller.

My fifteen years of video store experience gave him confidence in me. A week later I met Reed Hastings, who had offered to fund the concept of a DVD rental and sales store on the internet. Reed was another super smart guy but in a very different way from Marc. Reed could read people and what made them tick, and more importantly whether they could get on the bus that Marc was driving and that Reed would initially be funding.

Reed also asked me about the concept and customer interest. This time I was a bit more prepared, but even so my thoughts, while intriguing, were filled with errors and omissions. He also asked me about the studios and their reactions. I filled him in on the early battles in the video rental industry that guaranteed the right to buy and sell and rent DVDs legitimately purchased from authorized distributors. We finished lunch and Marc right there and then offered me a job. Now of course I wanted to seem more thoughtful since the office would be a good hour-and-a-half drive from my home and I had my stores, NSI, my trade association work, and three kids and a wife. I asked them to give me a week to think about it.

When I came home that day to discuss joining Netflix with my wife and kids, I tried to remember all the family movies I had seen where the dad runs a big momentous decision by the family followed by vigorous debate, some smart questions, and a final agreement. I sat them down and talked to them. It was not like the movies. There were blank looks from all. My kids were both not interested and dubious of this idea of mailing DVDs to your home. They all said, almost in unison, "Dad, that is the stupidest idea we have ever heard." My wife was willing to go along, so long as I wasn't investing any money. In the end there was no consensus, just "Okay, Dad, if you think it is a good idea then, well, we really don't care." I learned that evening just how motivating and compelling trying to prove your wife and kids wrong would be. In fact, in the following five years it served as perpetual motivation when things were tough.

Now at the same time NSI was starting to pick up steam, especially after the trade show. We were getting a flood of video chains signing up with us and things were looking up. I really wanted to work with Marc, but I also wanted to spend more time on NSI. So when the time came to reply to Marc's offer I said, "How about I become a part-time consultant?" Marc was fine with that, knowing that I would always be ready to help with connections and advice at a rate of $10,000 per month.

A few months later, when it became more clear that NSI was not going to go anywhere, which Marc had told me a few months earlier, I realized that I had made a mistake and that full time at Netflix was my best option. So over the Christmas holiday, I spoke several times with Marc and we agreed that I would come on as vice president of business development at the end of January 1998, and I would get stock options for 1.5 percent of the company. I would also fill in for other work that needed to be done including acquiring movies and negotiating with studios, and I would join the executive leadership team of about seven people. We set up an office in Scotts Valley, California, in an old bank. The bank vault was going to be where we would store our inventory.

Around this time, we worked on an iconic name for the company. Marc had a whiteboard in his office and people wrote possible names up there, like NowShowing and CinemaCenter. Marc was a fan of Rent.com. My recollection is that one of the more popular suggestions was "Movies-by-Mail"—very literal, and a name that would certainly have made it hard for the company to expand into what it eventually became. We eventually settled on Netflix— short, descriptive, catchy, and forward-looking (as opposed to anything with "by mail" in it). So now the new company had a name.

There was a lot of stress associated with my new role with Netflix. I was able to maintain the image that I knew exactly what I was doing, but deep inside my own brain I was worried that I really didn't know jack shit about actually operating in a business like this. I often would make suggestions and be quickly informed how naïve my idea was, how the idea had been done fifty times before and always failed. This took its toll. I would come home exhausted, with little energy for my family, and I know I drank far too much as a way to cope.

My first job with Netflix was to get out there and set up purchasing agreements with distributors. I set things up with Ingram and with Video Products Distributors, which could supply major studio movies, as well as a few smaller suppliers including an Indian movie supplier. And with that, in the first quarter of 1998, we started building a rental library of around a thousand titles with one copy of each title, and a few extra copies for the current week's new releases.

Being a pretty lean organization, we wanted to keep costs low. So I asked my three kids, who all knew video stores really well, to take the thousand or so new DVDs and prep them for rental. The deal was I would either pay them or buy them a new PlayStation or Xbox system. Their job was to remove the shrink-wrap from the case, remove the disk, insert it in a rental sleeve, and add the appropriate title and barcode to the outside of the sleeve. I am still in dispute with my kids Joaquin, Paloma, and Emiliano regarding whether they were properly compensated.

The first week our rental service was open to the public was in April 1998. That week's new theatrical releases were *L.A. Confidential* and *Boogie Nights*, both Warner releases. Despite our having no customers, the Warner rep, Issie Boorstein, convinced me to buy 240 copies of each title. In exchange he would pay for a full-page co-op Netflix ad in the *San Francisco Chronicle*, which would have cost around $25,000 otherwise. Of course, most readers of the *Chronicle* had no clue what Netflix was nor what mail-order DVD rental was. The only part that they understood was mail-order DVD purchases. Our pricing model was $4.99 for a one-week rental plus 99 cents for shipping and handling. You paid extra-day charges after that. In addition, we sold all the movies at cost or slightly below cost, trying to match Walmart pricing. We quickly learned that that is never a good long-term strategy, since Walmart's pricing is below our wholesale cost.

We were building a retail store on the internet and trying to do everything to replicate the experience you would get walking into a store, such as getting recommendations from one of the many knowledgeable clerks, being able to read the titles and descriptions, seeing who the directors and stars were, and hopefully taking all that plus your mood into account in choosing the perfect film to bring home to your family or to watch on your own. We struggled with how to do the same things that video stores do with inventory, regarding which titles to add to the library and how many copies of each title to purchase in forecasting demand.

In those days you had to place your order for DVDs with the studios a month in advance. How could you increase your copy depth to meet what you expected to be growing user base and need? At the beginning you have no real valid data for predicting how effective growth techniques such as advertising, word of mouth, and PR would be, so to be prepared we did our estimates and then bumped the numbers up some to be safe. As

Marc would tell me when I would show him the costs, "We have more to lose if we do not have enough of the titles people want than if we buy too many." We would often discuss the advantage that Blockbuster has with its brightly lit corner stores reminding customers that "We have fun here." How would we attract that kind of attention on the internet, where you have to literally go find us and then remember to order a few days before the video was at your home ready to view?

These were the days when we joined the "pop-up" bandwagon looking for how to trigger a compelling message in a pop-up keyed to the demographics of a prospective customer. The easy part was, around 80 percent of households rented movies; the negative was that barely 5 percent owned a DVD player.

There is no comparison to today's world where an airline search for Spain on Kayak will generate a message, emails, and ads that follow you everywhere about hotels and travel in Madrid. We were in a constant state of testing and analyzing, then fine-tuning and relaunching, and then doing it all over again. The whole idea of staying at the top of potential and existing customers' minds became one we focused on a lot. We thought, how can we get presence inside the customer's home in order to remind them to rent a DVD from us at Netflix.com?

With the prices of DVD players dropping dramatically from over $500 in 1996 and 1997 down into the $300 range by the time we got to 1998, we planned and executed a strategy that would insert in every DVD player sold in the United States a license-plate-sized coupon that looked like a movie ticket, offering free rentals at Netflix. Most of our offers were eight free rentals, and you received a code on the coupon that you would enter at Netflix when you signed up. We made deals with almost every player manufacturer: Sony, Panasonic/Matsushita, Pioneer, JVC, and many others.

The player manufacturers loved it, because their biggest barrier to sales was consumers saying, "Okay, I love the quality and the small format, and I see that I can buy DVDs in lots of places, but no retailers are renting DVDs. So if I could only be assured that I could rent near my home, I would buy this." Netflix was the solution no matter where you lived in the United States. And the free rentals were an added value to the sale worth $25 or more in the eyes of the customer. Our costs were printing and shipping and paying for the DVDs to rent, and mailing costs. Our goal, of course, was to convert those free rental customers to long-term paying renters.

But none of these ideas raised our awareness and visibility enough. Marc was getting concerned. I remember Marc opining one day that there are thousands of brightly lit Blockbuster Video stores within just a few blocks of almost everyone in the country. You can walk in and get a movie minutes later. Who needs to wait for a disk to come in the mail after two or three days?

We needed a stunt. Something outrageous enough to generate ink, but close enough to our rental model to get us actual customers. And in September, I learned two things that made all the difference.

First, I discovered a way to create DVD master disks from video in hours, rather than months. An old friend, Arthur Mrozowski, a Polish émigré, told me about a company called Mindset, headquartered in Sunnyvale, California, with a new technology that could create a DVD master in just a few hours.

And second, the nation was transfixed by a scandal involving a president who'd apparently fooled around with an intern named Monica Lewinsky. President Bill Clinton's grand jury testimony would be aired publicly. Here's a fact you may not know: anything that's created by the US government is in the public domain, with no copyright. That includes the president of the United States talking about what he did or didn't do with a young intern in a blue dress.

My friend Arthur and I conceived a plan. A friend at KTVU, a San Francisco TV station, would record the testimony on a large professional-format recorder. We'd make a DVD out of it with chapter links so you could go directly to President Clinton's definition of sex. And we'd sell it cheap (we ended up pricing it at two cents). We'd get lots of media and lots of sign-ups on the Netflix site. And then we'd have customers to email about our DVD rentals.

My job was to get the DVD copies made. Our PR person TE's job was to line up the media. She did great, lining up a front-page story for the *Wall Street Journal*. That was the plan, but things don't turn out to be as simple as they look on paper. Ideas are easy. Execution is a bitch.

At five a.m. on Tuesday morning, September 22, 1998, Arthur and I picked up the tape with the testimony recorded on it and drove to the Mindset office, where, for the first time, I saw the process of mastering a DVD. It had been advertised as quick. It was not. They started by converting the tape to a digital file and laying it down on a disk image at seven a.m.; that process finished at one a.m. on Wednesday morning. But finally, I had the "silver master" disk in my hand. We tested it in six DVD players in Mind-set's facility.

It worked on the Panasonic and Toshiba and two others. But on the Sony and Pioneer DVD players—nothing but static. DVD mastering was a little more subtle than it appears.

Still, a zen disruptor persists, never giving up. I hadn't slept but remained cool and confident, though it's a good thing no one smelled my underarms. And Arthur said he could fix it. By day-break, Marc was calling again. He called every couple of hours. I told him to put off the *Journal* and the other media and we'd be in touch soon.

Later Wednesday afternoon, we had a second silver master. We slipped it into the Sony player. Success! But it wouldn't work on the Panasonic. Arthur said he knew how to fix the encoding and started again. I'd drunk enough coffee to keep a rhino awake. I waited.

At four a.m. on Thursday, we finally got a master disk that worked on all six DVD players. I called Marc with the thumbs-up; he posted the two-cent offer on the Netflix site. We drove to the manufacturing facility in Fremont and rang the bell. An Asian guy answered; he spoke no English. He took us to a bare, warehouse-like room full of machines, blank disks on spindles, and other Asian guys who also spoke no English.

Sometimes creativity strikes at odd times. Other times, you need to summon it on demand. I showed the guy the disk and, knowing that about 100 DVDs fit on a spindle, I wrote down how many spindles of DVDs we needed to be replicated. He got it. And a few hours later, I was walking out of there with a few thousand newly printed disks. There were no fancy graphics on the disks, no time for that—all it said, in tiny misspelled letters on a ring at the center of the disk, was "Cliton DVD."

I rushed over to our Netflix office, where the company meeting was going on. I looked like shit, but they were all cheering madly at the sight of the Clinton Testimony DVDs. TE, the PR person, re-contacted the newspapers and said, it's on. And I marched over to the mailing location, which was in the disused bank vault (got to keep those valuable DVDs safe, after all), and they started printing out mailing labels for the envelopes.

With the help of Arthur ferrying disks a thousand at a time from the Fremont plant, we shipped our DVDs. As a result of articles in the *Wall Street Journal* and elsewhere, we got five thousand names and emails. Our "no customers" problem was solved, and we were off and running.

But success is not a onetime accomplishment. You must never rest on your laurels. I learned this the hard way when, a few days later, a staffer pointed me to an online DVD forum where people were making strange comments about our Clinton DVD.

Apparently, a few people got more than their two cents' worth. Sure enough, a couple of those spindles that Arthur had brought over had slightly different tiny letters on the hub of the disk. Customers who received these DVDs saw not a politician talking, but a hard-core Japanese porno feature called *The Lonely Widow*. And we had no way to know which customers got the porno and which got the president.

Chagrined, we did the only thing we could: we sent out a notice telling people to mail back the disks if they got the wrong DVD, and we'd replace it with the president, just as promised.

After all, those five thousand customers were the seed corn that was going to launch our business.

But I'll be damned, not a single customer ever complained or returned any of those disks.

In those early sink-or-swim days of Netflix, we began building the infrastructure for a magic formula: if you could understand what each individual subscriber wanted to watch, and when and how they wanted to watch it, you could win the love and loyalty of millions of consumers worldwide.

But still Netflix was an afterthought, not your first choice for entertainment. What could we do?

These marketing programs—with the new DVD machine buyers and the Clinton DVD—made Netflix synonymous with DVD rental and brought us many customers. But once the free rentals were used up, not many stayed around to pay. This problem loomed larger and larger and by early 1999, it became a central topic of the Tuesday executive meetings that ran from nine to noon.

The question was, what do we do? Was it a problem with the way we were attracting new customers, or was it the place we were getting them from? Was our product attractive enough to compete with the expanding availability of DVD rental at video stores? Was our pricing wrong? Was the problem the one-to-three-day wait time to get your movie?

In fact, it was all of those.

I had successfully made the transition from video store owner to start-up executive. Netflix was part of me, and I was part of it. So this was my problem, along with everyone else's. How do you find a solution that fixes all those faults in one smooth package? We spent until September 1999 trying to figure that out.

TAKEAWAY

One of the most awesome phenomena is when the perfect mix of people come together on the right project at the right time. Many people in business refer to "getting the right people in the seats on the bus" as an important challenge for founders to successfully manage. Netflix brought together, at the right moment, a mission designed and built by that almost unimaginable team that laid the foundation for a world-changing business.

[5]

HOW NETFLIX MONTHLY SUBSCRIPTIONS TRANSFORMED THE VIDEO BUSINESS

Samma Ajiva (Right Livelihood)
Once we understand the path and have worked out the details
so that they function in unison, we can concentrate on growth.

By now I had fully bought into Netflix. This was my chance to make something notable happen, and I was in the thick of solving the company's problems.

We were moving fast and slow at the same time. We had built a working online video rental and sales store. You could set up your account with a credit card and a mailing address. You could rent a film for a week for $4.99 or buy one at a cost that rivaled Walmart.

Our strategy was to build a large pool of DVD consumers who got enormous value and would be open to our next DVD offering. The eventual plan was to use DVD rental as a first step in building an entertainment portal that would attract consumers for movie news, cinema tickets, and DVD sales and rentals, and generate revenue off those eyeballs. We didn't exactly know what that would be, but we had this aura of confidence that came from working with incredibly diverse and creative people all focused on "figuring it out."

I felt like the real lucky one. I had no tech background other than always being the early tech consumer. In 1975, I had purchased and installed a fifteen-foot diameter motorized satellite dish, before satellite TV was a commercial product. I bought the first beta video cameras in 1982, the Elcaset high-performance audiocassette player, the pre-Casio Timex digital watch—you name it, I bought it. And at Netflix I was surrounded by highly educated and experienced start-up and tech pioneers who actually understood how all those gadgets worked. Every meeting for me was like a Harvard Business School class and I was eating it up.

Every Tuesday, Marc Randolph held an executive leadership meeting that ran a few hours. Each leader was expected to update the rest on significant accomplishments and issues from the previous week. My job was evolving. I began with content acquisition and operations plus introductions to the entertainment companies. Then I handed operations over to our COO, Tom Dillon, and spent more time with DVD manufacturers and retailers in an effort to use their marketing muscle to promote Netflix, a strategy Marc called OPM, or using Other People's Money. OPM was working really well. I continued and enhanced the early partnerships Marc had created with Sony, and I expanded our promotional plan to include manufacturers of 95 percent of all DVD players.

As I described in the previous chapter, the DVD manufacturers inserted our coupon on top of the player in the box so that when the customer opened the box to install the player, the first thing they would see is our coupon. This was perfect since the consumer's first question was, "What shall I watch?" At this time Blockbuster did not rent DVDs in every store, and where they did it was a very small selection.

Because the electronics stores found this to be a valuable sales benefit, the salespeople would also tell the prospective buyer about Netflix. The manufacturers not only inserted the coupon for free but also promoted Netflix in store, in print ads, and wherever they could. The cost to us was supplying the free rentals, all in the hope that many of those free-trial customers would convert to paying for the service.

Our problem was how we distinguished ourselves from the competition, which at that point was in only two facets of value: home delivery and an extensive catalog of long tail titles. Many customers were lukewarm about that, since they said they actually liked going to video stores that were typically near their home or other stores they were visiting anyway and most customers just wanted the big hit titles.

Our other big challenge was, how do you give the manufacturers all the same program when you have one or two big players and a lot of smaller ones? At the time Sony dominated the electronics market in everything: TVs, Walkmans, and DVD players. Of course they wanted a special deal.

That deal would increase our exposure in Sunday newspaper entertainment sections where Sony historically had full back-page ads promoting the latest DVD player and Sony movies. Their proposal was that if we bumped the eight free rentals to ten and paid for up to three new Sony DVDs to own for the new player buyer, we would get prime placement in Sunday newspaper ads, on retail store shelves, and more. Sony would pay for the first title, which was a James Taylor concert DVD that every player buyer would receive, and then, depending on the cost of the player, the buyer could select between one and three DVDs among hundreds of titles to own, all at Netflix's cost.

The redemption would be by old-fashioned mail. Once the customer registered their DVD player purchase online, we sent them the list of titles. Then they filled it out, including the bar-code of the player they purchased, and mailed it to us, after which we would mail them their DVDs.

Being relative newbies to the coupon redemption business, we did not anticipate the ways customers could exploit our incomplete terms and conditions that did not say "one per customer." Bottom line, we had to purchase several million dollars' worth of DVDs to fulfill thousands of duplicate coupon redemptions. We had no choice but to fulfill the redemptions.

Up until this time Marc was the president, but soon after this fiasco, Reed and Marc announced that from that point forward, Reed would come in as a full-time CEO running operations, finance, and engineering, and Marc would be president, managing the front of the store, website, content, marketing, and customer service.

You could tell that Marc was hurt, but he and Reed had an amazing relationship built on "radical honesty," and as always Marc put the company first. This was a great lesson that I took to heart. Several times in the future I would realize how Marc must have felt. As Reed would say, this was a company, not a family.

Many, many times in the future as I gained more responsibility and authority, I would struggle with that balance of loyalty, teamwork, and the cold reality of the needs of the enterprise.

During this time I learned a lot from Patty McCord, Netflix's head of human resources. Marc and Reed had brought her over from their previous company, and we shared a card table workspace for more than a year. During that time, she developed a whole culture for Netflix, based on the importance of valuing individuals for who they are, what they want, and what they are passionate about. Sitting there was like having a VIP pass to hearing how the whole culture was formulated in her mind. Patty eventually wrote her own book on corporate culture, titled *Powerful*.

I believe it was Patty who had the sense and the strength to get the basic concepts of the Netflix culture embedded into the heart and soul of the company. These included unlimited vacation time and no micromanaging. Reed's contribution was a plan to let the bottom 10 percent go every year and ensure that everyone fulfills their expected objectives when they are expected and no later. Patty taught me the importance of diversity at every level of the company, especially at the top; she taught me to respect different and counter opinions; and she taught me how to identify the characteristics in prospective employees that would bring you "onto the bus."

I was commuting down every Monday from Marin County north of San Francisco to Scotts Valley near Santa Cruz and returning home on Wednesday or Thursday. From 1998 on, as the Silicon Valley dot-com bubble grew, so did the commute. It expanded from an hour to an hour and a half. My solution was to leave earlier and to listen to books on tape: history, language, and college courses. Some were so entrancing that I would arrive in the Netflix parking lot and not get out of my car for fifteen minutes or more.

Some Tuesday nights Marc and his wonderful wife, Lorraine, would invite me to tag along on their wine-tasting dinners with a few other people, but generally I would while away the time in my hotel room.

Once Tom Dillon was recruited to run operations, Netflix's logistics ran incredibly smoothly. Previously Tom had led operations for the data storage company Seagate. I was now able to spend more time with DVD distributors and studios. There were four major distributors in the United States; the top two were Ingram and VPD. I had used both while running my video stores, and both were good. They each carried all the major studio product and were willing to work with you on obtaining co-op advertising money from the studios. While they were risk averse, they both were willing to extend sixty-day credit terms based on my track record as a video store owner. Since typically in the rental business your cost of goods averaged 40 percent of revenue, having two months to pay meant we could use upcoming revenue to pay the bills, which reduced our funding needs by a ton.

Meanwhile the exec team was pushing to get the studios to consider a revenue-sharing model, which would have the added benefit of protecting us from overbuying and allow us to guarantee, to a certain extent, that we could meet demand. That was really the conundrum in the rental business. More than anything you were "managing disappointment." You couldn't afford to buy enough copies of a movie, whether it was on VHS at a wholesale cost of $70 or even on DVD at a wholesale cost of $18, because within a couple of weeks, or around $12 of income, 90 percent of the demand for that movie would vanish and you were left with a used movie to sell for a few dollars.

I noticed that many of our customer service contacts were coming from Silicon Valley engineers, many of whom were of Indian background. This reminded me of the local Indian grocery store that did a brisk business in renting Indian VHS titles to their customers. It didn't take long before I tracked down a guy who represented about six hundred Hindi and Urdu titles, which I licensed and launched as Netflix's first real niche content play. The word of mouth and loyalty this engendered with super influential tech consumers went a long way. You might say this was a small foray into exclusive content, since, in effect, no one else carried this selection.

Tom had moved our "bank vault" inventory room to a vast space next to the San Jose USPS hub. We hadn't yet figured out how to barcode the disk itself, and so the inventory consisted of shelves and shelves filled with shoebox-size open cardboard boxes with a hundred or so DVDs per box. They were all in thin paper sleeves with the title and barcode on the sleeve. They were stored not alphabetically, but by a number code, based on the order of when we acquired the inventory. When gathering an order for three titles, the warehouse person could spend ten minutes walking around the storage space.

We were getting plenty of exposure. Dot-coms were hot. The challenge was that after returning the last of the free rentals, most customers went back to their Blockbuster or Hollywood Video store. We couldn't replicate that shining *Blockbuster* on nearly every high-traffic street corner. What could we do to stay top of mind? We tried pop-ups on the internet, which were in their infancy and annoying. We created a plastic Netflix-branded DVD rack you could place on your TV. Nothing seemed to work and we were starting to get desperate for an improvement to our model that would truly convert our customers.

One thing that *was* working was the increasing volume of Netflix's iconic red envelope mailings. Thousands were mailed every day to homes around the United States. Many arrived in one or two days, with just a few arriving on the third day after ordering. First postal workers, then almost everyone, noticed that red envelopes were showing up everywhere. The envelope had four panels with our logo and a few mailing instructions but mostly blank space. Why not sell advertising space on the envelope?

The big innovation began one day in the summer of 1999, as the exec team was touring the San Jose warehouse and discussing the failure of all these Band-Aids applied to create real stickiness for our service. I remember Reed looking at all the boxes of DVDs and turning to the seven or so of us and saying, "What are all these DVDs doing here in the warehouse where they aren't doing us any good? Shouldn't they be at our customers' homes?" And with that, the leaders each went off to see how we could move the inventory as close to the customers sitting in their homes ready to watch. I believe the history of all sales has been, the faster you can satisfy a customer need from the moment they want your product to the time they can use it, the more you succeed.

This is where Marc and the store team shone. First they came up with the subscription concept that would give each customer four movies of their choice to have at home ready to watch any time (solving the immediacy issue); they could return them one at a time and within days receive another movie of their choice. Marc's team also came up with the queue that the customer would use to list films they wanted to see, so when Netflix received one of the four DVDs back it would pick the next in-stock movie from the customer's queue and send it right away (solving the shopping fatigue problem). We delivered all of this for the cost of about four movies at Blockbuster.

The big, big win was "No Late Fees." Blockbuster was a $5-billion-a-year business in the United States known for entertainment, yet it was in the top ten most hated brands because of fees it charged when you returned a movie late. With our queue system, there were never any late fees.

The system for subscriptions and the queue were built in a matter of months and were ready to launch in September 1999. But there were a couple of big problems. Since every time we mailed another DVD we incurred about $1.20 in shipping and supplies, and since most DVDs cost around $18, what would happen if the average subscriber saw fifteen movies a month, which you could easily do if you mailed back all four movies every six days? We would spend $18 just on mailing not to mention cost of goods and labor on what was a $19.95 monthly subscription. And we were very convinced consumers would not accept anything with higher pricing.

With that fear in mind, we launched this new Netflix subscription to a small number of customers. Since there was no social media at the time, it was mostly a stealth product launch, which gave us four or five months to measure consumption.

By January it was clear that on average, consumption was acceptable at between six and seven DVDs a month. That brought on probably the biggest and hardest decision the Netflix leadership team had to make. Do we offer both our weekly à la carte rental service, which was doing tens of millions of dollars in revenue, and add in the subscription, or do we kill the à la carte rentals and just offer subscription? And what about sales of DVDs? Do we continue that as a service and to keep our customers out of our competitors' stores? And what about all the credits stored on our customers' accounts for free rentals based on their DVD player purchase?

I was learning so much about the strategic decision-making process from Reed, Marc, Patty, Tom, and other executives, including the CFO, Barry McCarthy, and the CMO, Leslie Kilgore. Reed, as always, made decision-making as close to a science as anyone I ever met. "Let's do what we can do better than anyone else" was his guidance, and not for the first time. "No one else is doing DVD subscription. It's working. Let's only do that and stop doing à la carte rental and sales." And with that, the decision was made.

You can imagine the complexity of the timeline and the communication both externally and internally. The plan involved product, engineering, marketing, legal, finance, and HR. I too had a role in communicating it to our partners.

Basically, it worked. The hockey stick growth had begun.

Around this time in our lead-up to filing to go public for the first time, we began building out a "portal" strategy. In other words, we would become *the* place for all things entertainment. Movies, reviews, showtimes, tickets, gossip, news, et cetera. Our value and earnings would come from advertising based on growing traffic, and DVD rental would be just one of many traffic builders. To that end we hired the former head of ad sales at Egghead Software to build a sales department. And then the dot-com bubble burst in April 2001. We pulled our IPO filing and went back to a business built on a huge DVD rental subscriber base and not on traffic.

Soon the ad sales department was let go and ad sales shut down, and we renewed our focus on fast delivery. The company became obsessed with shortening the time between placing the order and receiving the DVD. Even then we knew that some form of digital delivery would be better than relying on the USPS, but in those days there was nothing close to the bandwidth needed, nor were there smart TVs to receive a digital movie, nor would the studios risk the potential piracy. But that mantra of faster and faster delivery drove many major decisions for us.

Once the subscription was launched, Reed and Marc had brought me into a meeting to discuss the future management of content acquisition. Reed made it clear that I would have to move to Los Angeles and set up shop there if I was to continue managing content. I was really enjoying the creative aspects of creating strategic business relationships and the freedom and flexibility of my role as vice president of business development and strategic partnerships. I saw DVD purchasing as boring and more of an accountant role. (Little did I know how interesting licensing, greenlighting, and eventually producing movies, documentaries, and TV series would become.)

I was also having personal problems at home, so after one day of thinking about it, I told Reed, "No, I want to stay in business development." He asked me for recommendations for content buyers who lived in Los Angeles. A month later, in early December 1999, I was attending the annual Video Hall of Fame event in L.A., and I scheduled a few minutes to meet with my friend Ted Sarandos to tell him about this opening. Ted had a long history managing video rental stores in Phoenix, and then running the western region for a major distributor called East

Texas Distributors (ETD). He had recently given up on a project trying to cobble together a network of video stores, then take them public under the name of Video City.

Besides being a very solid guy, Ted was also one of the most knowledgeable and connected entertainment execs I had ever met. You wouldn't want to bet money and play six degrees of separation with Ted. So Ted and I sat down and I shared with him how amazing the Netflix team was. While skeptical, he agreed to let me throw his name in the ring for consideration. The following week at the next Tuesday leadership meeting, I excitedly told the team about Ted and why I thought he was the right guy to run content, and the team was open to it. Later that day with the hot sun beating down, I sat in my Taurus on my cell phone telling Ted the good news.

I thought he would be more excited. "Will this internet wave continue?" he wanted to know. Forty-five minutes later he agreed to come for the interview. Reed, Marc, and everyone loved Ted, and he started soon after in early 2000. And in fact, much of the success of Netflix in the years following was a result of Ted launching Red Envelope, Netflix's first foray into content—even when that program failed, they resurrected exclusive content and are spending more than $18 billion annually on it.

As you may remember, in April 2001, the market totally fell apart after the dot-com bubble burst. In the five years leading up to that fateful month, almost anything connected to the internet saw its stock price rise, even though many of the offerings had little or no real underlying value behind them. There were all these companies that were worth millions of dollars on paper but sold the digital equivalent of promises and sock puppets. But once the market realized they were worthless, things got a lot tougher for going public. So we had to bide our time for a few months.

Around this time I was invited to give a presentation about Netflix to a meeting in Palm Springs of the leaders of the cassette and disk manufacturing organization. I prepped with Ted Sarandos, as I knew that he knew many of the members, and I suggested we do this together on stage. I knew this would be a great way for these folks to get a better understanding of how Netflix worked and what opportunities there might be. Since home delivery of movies was a relatively unknown model and because we were especially proud of our innovative red envelope, I thought during the slides where we showed our growth we would do a small demo. So we set up a mailbox on the stage, the kind you might see in front of a home in the suburbs. We also made a large flat cutout made to look like the side of a USPS delivery van. After showing on the screen the vast selection and how a customer would order, we demo'd inserting the DVD in the envelope, giving it to the USPS, and delivering to the mailbox, and we even showed the return process. What I failed to notice was that the crowd of around three hundred people were joined by their spouses for dinner while Ted and I droned on about this company that they clearly cared nothing for. What's worse is we were standing between dinner and a night on the town. About twenty minutes before we would finish, I started hearing talking and lots of rustling seats. Ignoring that was disastrous; within five minutes the wives mostly were heckling us to finish. Incredibly embarrassed, I looked at Ted and then, addressing the audience, said, "And that's all I can share about Netflix." The crowd clapped and then quickly disappeared. I never forgot how important it is to understand who you are presenting to and be respectful of what they want.

My years of working in video stores, talking about films, making recommendations, determining price points, doing merchandising, and planning promotions gave me a good understanding of how consumers think about selecting a movie to watch and, just as important, what makes them come back. Was it the enjoyment of the right movie, the right movie for their mood, the shopping experience, or the price? These were all components of an overall experience, one that was difficult to transition from a retail store to an online site. Movie selection was one of the most challenging things to move online. How do you merchandise the film when your library is five times bigger than in a store? How do you guide the customer to great films that, in a retail store, the customer would walk by on their way to the back wall that carried the big new hits? And how do you replicate store clerk picks or store recommendations?

At Netflix we came up with Cinematch, an algorithm based on collaborative filtering that recommended films that had been liked by other people with the same viewing profile as you. It worked but it was an imperfect system, as from time to time we would recommend films like Jack Nicholson's frightening *The Shining* to customers who liked *Willy Wonka and the Chocolate Factory*.

I had tested many merchandising and promotional programs at my video stores and found that you needed to somehow connect to what was top of mind at that moment for a customer. So stories in the news about China would create interest in films that took place in China. I have always been a fan of indie film cinema and small art-house theaters, so I launched a project to test our ability to use Cinematch data to drive subscribers to the movie theater to see small films with no real marketing budget. I would start by identifying a movie opening the following week in the San Francisco Bay Area, then pick three DVD titles that were similar to that title, and then promote the art-house film to our subscribers who lived within ten miles of the theater and liked two of the three comp titles. The results were amazing. Among those customers, 7 percent said they went to the movie and 70 percent of those said they enjoyed or loved the film. Even better, most brought someone with them and most recommended the film to somebody else.

Our director of analytics, Joel Mier, taught me more about the science of measuring intent than anyone I had met up until then. I doubt if Joel knew his impact on me and how I would take those lessons in helping design Redbox's offerings later in my career. Joel's group was regularly running a series of experiments on the website: focus groups and customer sentiment all designed to set direction and educate the entire Netflix team on what our subscribers wanted more of. One test I watched Joel do for amusement was to drop various size coins in the men's urinals at the Netflix offices in Los Gatos: pennies, nickels, dimes, and quarters. I am proud to say I never pulled out a coin, but I was surprised when he told me that quarters never lasted. It is that illogical aspect of forecasting interest that was hard to grasp but so important. Once again I'm reminded of Nobel Prize–winning economist Richard Thaler and his work on understanding how consumers sometimes choose illogically and even against their own self-interest.

While all this was going on, I was also spending a lot of my time on what I believed would be a "big deal" for Netflix. Best Buy was the best and biggest seller of both DVD players and DVD movies. They would pick three product programs each year to focus their stores and sales on. For products that were part of those three focus programs, every store employee was trained to push the product, store signage promoting them was all over the store, and their very sophisticated point-of-sale systems, including checkout registers, would integrate prompts about the program into every possible sale. After about six months of flying back and forth from San Francisco airport to their headquarters in Minneapolis, I managed to get Netflix included as one of the focus programs. That meant that every time a customer purchased anything in the entertainment department, the sales clerk would ask them, "How would you like a free trial at Netflix?" If you said yes, the clerk would ask for your email address and request that you click a box on the credit card authorization, and a few minutes later you received a welcome from Netflix by email and were asked to pick a few movies. Within days your first batch of movies would arrive. Best Buy got bounties per conversion based on when that customer actually paid, plus Netflix stock. For a while, Best Buy generated 17 percent of all new subscribers, with most of the balance coming from DVD player box coupons.

That deal was so consequential that it made a big impression on Reed. He said, half joking, "We will have to get key man insurance for you." That felt great. And I tried to live up to it by finding more and bigger deals.

Despite our hockey stick growth curve, now that Netflix was all in on subscriptions, we were experiencing awareness and adoption that was minuscule relative to the size of the DVD market. DVD was the quickest of all electronic products to be adopted as a percentage of households in the United States even faster than televisions, stereos, and VCRs, and it would soon take over all of the market share from VHS. Netflix awareness was low because, unlike today, going to the internet was not a daily task and there was no social media, so the chance that a prospective customer would find out about us was mostly driven by luck.

I saw my overall mission at Netflix as identifying sources for new subscribers via partnerships. Marc was always using the code OPM or Other People's Money as a way to denote strategic allies. These allies typically were selling hardware like DVD players or home theater systems and so benefited when their prospective customer could get access to a wide range of content through Netflix. One of the new ideas that Marc and I had hatched up was building and installing automated kiosks that would essentially place mini-warehouses of Netflix DVDs in your local grocery store. We called it Netflix Express. Netflix Express kiosks would be installed in thousands of convenient shopping locations like grocery stores where 250 million Americans shopped weekly. The Netflix Express kiosks would be in our signature colors and would stand out at the entrance where everyone could see them. You could sign up as a new subscriber and pick your first three mov- ies—we had recently cut the subscription price and were allowing subscribers three disks per month. You'd pick up the movies from the machine right then and instantly start your subscription. And you could return and replace any DVD on your regular visit to shop for groceries, rather than wait on the postal service.

We made two big decisions early on. First, we decided to build a test kiosk that would be staffed by a Netflix employee to mimic what an automated kiosk could do. The theory was, let's figure out first if there is a business worth investing in before we have to design and build an automated kiosk. And we decided to test this in some grocery stores in a suburb of Las Vegas where we would get the benefit of a diverse demographic of customers who had moved to Vegas from all over the United States—in a market less likely to be in view of the press. I made a deal with the execs at the Smith's grocery chain, and by early 2002 we had a kiosk up and running.

Unfortunately, the consumer interest was *too* good, growing to around one thousand new subscribers added each week. After three months, because of the elimination of almost all barriers to consumption, these subscribers viewed an average of nineteen movies per month, as compared to six or seven for online subscribers. At that rate of use, it was no longer profitable for us. So I had a few kinks to work out.

About a month later, I heard from another large retail chain. Some guys from McDonald's contacted me about a similar program they were running. It was a group called McDonald's Ventures, a venture arm of McDonald's that owned Chipotle, Boston Market, and other businesses.

McDonald's had just had their first declining year in the company's history. They had just been rising like a rocket, and then suddenly, in 2002, sales started going down. The president of the company, Stan Greenberg, got a bunch of McDonald's people together from all over the world, and they put together a think tank in Bethesda, Maryland. Their job was to brainstorm on the question "How can we rejuvenate McDonald's?"

They had all kinds of ideas, including the very poorly selling Healthy Choices menus. But they also came up with the idea of providing Wi-Fi at McDonald's restaurants, so people could come in and do work there. They actually ended up getting paid a ton of money from fast-growing cellular providers by putting Wi-Fi antennas often housed inside their golden arches.

They also had the idea to rent DVDs at McDonald's restaurants. The idea came from a real estate guy in the McDonald's organization in France whose name was, no kidding, Jean Deaux (pronounced John Doe). Jean Deaux realized that they'd done really well on hit videos released in partnership with the children's menu. "Why don't we rent DVDs," he said, "and when customers have to return them, they'll smell the burgers and fries, *et voilà!*" The McDonald's project was to install DVD vending machines at their thirteen thousand US locations that would rent and sell DVDs. They would include promotions tied to drinks and meals and ideally increase traffic. He was right in that almost 25 percent of all return visits generated a sale.

I got introduced to the team at McDonald's in November 2002. The team was diverse, to say the least. They were led by a Swede, with a Russian marketing exec, a German real estate person, and an Australian ops executive. After my intro to the full team, I impressed them with Netflix's understanding of the market and explained that I thought Netflix could grow dramatically if McDonald's was promoting our subscription to the tens of millions of weekly restaurant goers.

This was my chance to finally prove that my kiosk idea from the 1980s could work. I was all excited. I walked everybody at Netflix through how this idea would work with McDonald's. People could pick up movie DVDs and also pick up and drop off their Netflix subscription DVDs at McDonald's. I thought it was a killer idea.

I was in for a shock. Everybody at Netflix laughed. They said, "We wouldn't touch McDonald's brand with a ten-foot pole!" The unspoken, underlying vibe was, we're a high-class Silicon Valley company, headed to the digital future. We'd never eat at Mc-Donald's. (This was in spite of the fact that their wives were taking their kids to Mickey D's for Happy Meals every day after school.)

This really pissed me off. In fact, it slammed me so hard it made me turn a dark corner inside. Where was I going in this? Were my ideas so outside the framework the others operated within that I should be laughed at?

Around this time, the stock markets seemed to be shaking off their fears of anything internet-related. As a result, Netflix was set to go public in May 2002, the first company to go public after the dot-com implosion.

Merrill Lynch was the bank taking us public. And the problem was, just like all dot-coms, Netflix was running out of money. Each month that went by got more and more desperate. At the time, our business was still just mailing movies.

Our stock went out at $15 a share. Before, in the run-up to that, all of us on the executive committee were advised to set up an automatic stock sales plan with a broker, covering the six months after the stock went public. The idea was that the sales were locked in, so no one could accuse us of buying or selling or holding based on inside information. It being my first time in this position, I created a poorly designed program that was more based on protecting against declining share price, as we had all experienced during the bubble bursting the year before, rather than thinking long term.

After all the dilutions, I owned just under 1 percent of the company with my cost basis being around five cents a share. This stupid plan I'd set up essentially mandated that as our stock fell, it would sell more and more of my stock. Our stock started totally cratering. The price per share went from $15 down to $9 between May and November.

The financial analysts had discovered my Netflix Express stealth project in Las Vegas, perhaps tipped off because Hollywood Video, the second-largest video rental chain, had a store in the same mall as one of our kiosks. The analysts were asking, "What is Netflix doing? We thought they were leading business into the future of digital delivery, not a physical store," with a kiosk being kind of a proxy for a store. I thought that maybe our stock was going down because investors aren't investing in a kiosk company when they have the future expectation of straight digital delivery.

Recall that back in 2002, there was almost no video content available on the internet. Studios would not license content for any kind of downloads or streaming for fear of piracy. We always knew that eventually we'd get to pure streaming; that's why we called it Netflix and not Movies-by-Mail. But the analysts were attacking the strategy behind Netflix Express, so Reed made me kill the program.

It was gut-wrenching for me to see Netflix Express get pulled, because I wanted to prove that my vending machine idea that failed in the eighties had actually been a good one. In 1982, it had just been too early, and twenty years later it still wasn't ripe yet.

Meanwhile, I couldn't sell my stock. This was going to be my first shot at real wealth. So around November 2002, when Reed had me close down Netflix Express, I started thinking, Just what do I do now? I was flummoxed, having to close down something I thought was one of the best things we had been doing as I saw the value of my stock starting to go down. The shares of Netflix that I owned would soon be worth something like tens of millions of dollars. At the time, it was three to four million: real money. So I knew I had to either quit or figure out a way to get out of the plan that controlled my stock sales. Marc Randolph, the cofounder and president, who had three successful companies prior to Netflix, decided to leave his position on the board and the company in November so that he could monetize some of his equity—and I had to wonder if I was on the same path.

I was unhappy, and I wanted to leave. And I guess it showed. Reed came to me a couple weeks later and said, "Listen. I think you have to go. I can tell you're not happy. And by the way, I don't think your demeanor and the way you operate will work in a big public company, which we're becoming. So it's best you leave. January 2003 will be your last month. And we will give you a year's salary as severance and allow your options to vest for the full year of 2003."

It was a shock but it made sense. But before the conversation ended, Reed pointed out, "However, you're really good in a lot of things. So I'd like to hire you back as a consultant, starting right away. I'll pay you twenty grand a month. I want you to go to Europe and Japan to determine whether Netflix should open there. Come back in a couple months and give us a report and we'll go from there."

I like to travel. I knew I'd love to go to Europe and Japan and explore all those places and possibilities. So off I went to Europe. While I had an interesting time there, I found that the video markets there were mostly porn! Only the UK had a lot of similarities to the United States, and so I recommended that Netflix expand into there, which they did. As it turned out, very shortly after they had opened in the UK, Amazon moved into England with a movies-by-mail service. Fearing the cost of competing with Amazon, Netflix immediately closed down its own service. Additionally, as this was in 2004, Netflix would be adding a movies-by-mail setup in a foreign country, further becoming entrenched in the physical world. Streaming was still four years away, but this long-range planning allowed Netflix to be nimble as it migrated away from the shipping of the DVD to streaming content over the internet.

I felt great about what I'd done for Netflix. I'd innovated on partnerships with everyone from Sony to Best Buy. I'd resurrected my kiosk idea, only to see it shot down, and my idea to partner with McDonald's was also rejected.

I was no longer part of the company I'd help build from an idea in Marc Randolph's head to a fast-growing public company. What was I going to do now?

------------------------------ **TAKEAWAY** ------------------------------

One of the most significant differences between success and failure is knowing what to do next. The process you establish that helps guide where to focus your resources is the basis for achieving the outcome that founders have envisioned. At Netflix I observed the almost perfect mix of instinct and analysis that is the dream of all companies new and old, large and small.

[6]

MCDONALD'S AND REDBOX

Samma Ditthi (Right Understanding)
We must take what we have learned in the right concentration
and apply it to the situation we are trying to improve or master.

was embarrassed, sad, angry, and disappointed about how things
had ended at Netflix. And I hadn't sold enough Netflix stock to
generate sufficient cash so that I didn't have a need for income. I
knew I had to find another position. As it turned out, I was about
to start another adventure that would allow me to prove myself as
a big-company executive—and to vindicate my kiosk idea.

Karma and connections have a funny way of emerging at
times. In February 2003, I reconnected with the guy who was
running the McDonald's venture group. Little did I know this
connection would drastically change the trajectory of my life.

His name was Gregg Kaplan. On my way back from checking out Netflix expansion opportunities in the UK, I called Gregg
to reconnect. He said, "Great! We're still in Bethesda, Maryland.
We've just bought a couple of DVD vending machines from a

manufacturer in Israel. Why don't you stop by on your way back from England and come and meet the group?"

I totally hit it off with Gregg. He's a Harvard MBA, with a degree in philosophy from the University of Michigan, a super smart guy. I'm always attracted to people I can learn from. Gregg was a perfect fit.

McDonald's Ventures had six Israeli-made DVD vending machines. They looked like military-made construction: eight feet wide in the front and seven and a half feet high, about four feet deep. No surprise, one of the engineers who manufactured them in Haifa was a former major in the Israeli military! They were essentially trying to be a video store in a box, but they weren't doing the job. People would walk past these machines and say, "Why would I use that when there's a beautiful Blockbuster right next door in the same parking lot?" For me, these were echoes of past comments about my Video Droid kiosk. McDonald's Ventures asked me if I'd consult for them. And I told Gregg, "Well, I'm also still consulting for Netflix," and he said, "That's fine, we just want you to advise us on how to build the business model, how to make this vending machine idea work."

So I started working with these guys at McDonald's Ventures. Of course, at the time, I had already had two video vending machine failures with my VHS vending machine idea in the eighties and then the Netflix Express idea that led to my leaving Netflix. McDonald's was my third opportunity to prove that vending machines could work.

I got back together with Gregg and said, "I really want to take on a more serious role with your group." Starting in April 2002, he hired me as the chief operating officer of what, at the time, believe it or not, was called TikTok Video. We knew that was not a good name, but that was the name they had picked out of the air. We had these six Israeli military machines, and Gregg's team who weren't really video salespeople. I think they were renting out six movies a day—on a good day!

Gregg's eclectic international band (although not his hires) were smart people who sometimes thought they knew everything. Maybe my advantage was that I didn't know anything except that things weren't working and we needed to try other approaches.

I could see that their pricing was too high, and they had hundreds of titles to choose from—too many. The whole package just wasn't attractive to consumers, and it wasn't working. Then I realized, this is a whole new environment. I believed wholeheartedly in the concept of the machines. I wondered what specific things we needed to implement to draw people to the video rental machines.

There seemed to be only one way to find out. I started tinkering with everything about them: the locations, the look, the pricing, the merchandising, the inventory selection, and all the possible variables. Tinkering was the way to find the magical formula for success, I thought.

And that's how I came to be known as Tinkerbell.

It was a little off-putting at first to be called Tinkerbell, but to be fair, tinkering with the machine was what I was good at. So Tinkerbell I became, and proud of it.

I set up this regimen of rigorous testing where we changed little things in each machine to try to see what worked and what didn't. We tried different locations: outside, inside, by the cash register, by the exit door. We tried lots of titles or few titles. We tried big displays of movie posters, we tried little art displays. We tried 99 cents a night, we tried $3 for five nights. We tried 'em all. But no single change in the offer worked until we found a magic combination.

What we found, I call the three legs of the stool. Like a stool, all three legs have to be exactly the right length. After Tinkerbell had beat up the variables for a while, we found the three-legged combination that worked. Location: right at the outside of the store, as you walk in and out. Video selection: limited, in fact, only sixty titles. Price point: 99 cents a night. And, mostly because Netflix had found this to be successful, we got rid of the hated late fee. Late fees are a nightmare and really hurt people sometimes as well. By making it 99 cents a night, it kind of simplified the customer's thought process to, okay, for every night I keep a movie, it's 99 cents.

So anyway, once my alter ego as Tinkerbell got the three legs of the stool all measured the same length, we went from half a dozen rentals a day to something like sixty rentals a day per location. It was just kind of magic. But the machine itself wasn't right yet. We had to ship it over from Israel; it weighed a ton. We were paying something like $15,000 for each machine, plus shipping, plus import duties and more. So we began looking for a better solution.

We ended up working with a company called DVDPlay that could make a workable machine that wasn't built like a tank. And we were off and running.

Of course, we needed a name for the company. We hired a company to come up with something better than TikTok Video. They came in and presented a whole bunch of names, including

C3, which stood for Convenience Cubed. The logo was a red cube and, as some pointed out in our review, the cube looked more like a red box. And that is how we ended up with that iconic name. What was even more compelling was that our prototype machine, which was sitting right there in the corner, was covered in this red metal shell.

The machines were the final piece of the puzzle I'd been Tinkerbelling with. Because we had already determined the three legs of the stool, the whole project just took off. The machines were very quickly doing thirty, forty, fifty grand a year in revenue. Not only that, testing at McDonald's was showing that we were raising the hamburger, fries, and soda sales at each McDonald's by about 4 percent! Because the stores average $2.5 million in sales a year, that was like a hundred grand, almost all profit. So more stores signed on, and eventually just under three thousand McDonald's locations had Redbox.

Meanwhile, McDonald's started turning around its business. Remember, the whole reason they got into this was that they had declining sales. They finally figured out why. It was the cleanliness of their bathrooms! McDonald's was not cleaning the bathroom frequently enough.

They had all these hundreds of millions that they had invested in the stores and so their stores were very uniformly nice. But in my opinion one of the major reasons McDonald's business was flat to declining was the steady increase of young adult male customers attracted by the football advertising theme and a full meal for five bucks—and those young adult males were messing up the bathrooms and cleaning crews weren't cleaning them fast enough. The traditional McDonald's customers were mothers with kids generally under ten years old and the mothers were seeing that the bathroom was such a mess, so they stopped going to McDonald's. McDonald's started cleaning the bathrooms on a more regular basis and business just started shooting up.

By the end of 2004, they had all these older McDonald's management types saying, "What do we need Redbox for?" So they said, "Listen, we'll fund you through 2005. But at the end of the year, you're either closing down or finding another investor." Gregg had actually gone directly to McDonald's CEO Charlie Bell and got his approval to raise money outside McDonald's, and there always was the chance that if we failed, McDonald's would continue to back us.

We faced another problem around the same time. The DVD-Play machines didn't have enough capacity to hold all the disks we needed. By this time, we had moved from Bethesda and were working from the McDonald's headquarters in Oak Brook, Illinois. We heard about a company called GetAMovie, just up the road in Schaumburg, north of Chicago. They had a machine that held up to six hundred disks or so, they said. It was a working machine with a touchscreen. Their engineer, Franz Kuehnrich, a super smart Austrian living in the United States, demo'd the machine for us. I was totally blown away. They already had built a relationship with an experienced contract manufacturer called Solectron in Creedmoor, North Carolina. They took us down there and we met the team. The machine was like a dream. It worked perfectly. We liked what we saw and agreed to acquire the company.

We had the demo machine that they had built brought up to our office. Two weeks later I was tinkering with the software and the machine, and I suddenly realized that we needed to do a lot more work to have a functional kiosk. I was pushing on the screen trying to make the robotics inside go get a movie and dispense it. The machine didn't always do what I expected. I mean, it was almost as if during the demo they had someone behind a curtain, watching the buttons we hit and making the machine work! I realized we had just bought this company with a super smart engineer and a great relationship with a manufacturer, but its actual development was in an embryonic state. We had a huge mountain to climb to be customer ready.

We had traded something around 5 percent of Redbox for an amazing engineer and a working relationship with a third-party manufacturer. Thankfully the team was ready to step up and quickly build out the balance of what was needed.

This is where I had to learn calmness working through my disappointment in the status of what we acquired. My natural reaction would have been to say "Fuck you" or something even more counterproductive. But I knew, at the same time, that my only way to get out of this and to repair this whole situation was to take what we had and try to make it work, try to motivate them to catch up with the schedule.

With Eric Hoersten's help we pulled it off. Eric was a brilliant, super-young chief technology officer (CTO). I actually hired him as a data analyst, which is a very junior technology role, but I made him CTO just because he learned so quickly. Over the next two months, doing eighteen-hour days nonstop, all of us in Creedmoor, we turned it into a crash project. We built six hundred machines by the end of April. We were installing them at the rate of fifteen to twenty a week.

However, we hit another roadblock. More need for calm. Every seventh transaction failed! A customer would rent a movie and then try to return it and it would get stuck in the machine, or the credit card failed, or the touchscreen didn't work, or a myriad of other issues. What I needed to learn was, how do you convince people to put in yet another couple months of eighteen-hour days to get this to work? I had to meet with families. I met with spouses and with kids, because these employees were saying, hey, my spouse just can't handle this.

It was a struggle, but we were able to get everybody to recommit. I remember describing to everybody that, basically, it's like an onion. Every time we solved a problem, we would peel a layer off the onion. And then there was another problem underneath. And then another problem and another problem. It was arduous and exasperating, yet invigorating as well. We were working as a team. And eventually, after two months of nonstop work, suddenly we got past the last layer of problems and to the core of the onion. The machine worked!

With a working machine, we still had to solve the problem of getting an investor, because McDonald's was losing patience. Gregg and I spent ten or eleven months going all over the United States talking to investors. And every one of them said, "Wait a minute, I thought digital is coming and DVD is just an interim thing and DVD rental is going away." No one would invest, not a single person, even though at this time we were doing $10 million in revenue and there was a clear path to profitability. We had all these orders, we had everything working, we had the machine working, we had the right product mix, and the software was working. But investors said, "Wait a minute, your business is going to be over in a few years."

At that time in 2005, we were just starting to put some machines in grocery stores. When I was doing Netflix Express I had built a good relationship with the executives at the Smith's grocery chain, headquartered in Salt Lake City. I went back to them and said, "Listen, now I have this company, Redbox. We're installing rental kiosks." They said, "Sure, put them in our stores in Las Vegas." So we had 680 machines at McDonald's and 20 in the Smith's grocery stores, and they were all doing well.

But we still could not get an investor. We only had a month and a half before the McDonald's deadline passed and we would have to close down.

One day, around that time, I was reading a trade magazine for supermarkets called *Supermarket News,* and there was an article about a company called Coinstar. In it, Peter Rowan, who was their head of business development, said that Coinstar had something like thirteen thousand locations in grocery stores. Coinstar was an ingenious invention of a Stanford student who couldn't figure out how to easily convert change into bills—you dumped your jars of coins into the machine and it spit out money, after keeping a fee, of course. Rowan said Coinstar wanted to own the fourth wall in grocery stores, meaning that wall as you go out past the cash registers, where the Rug Doctor machine and all those kinds of things are. I called him, and within two weeks we had convinced Coinstar to buy 47 percent of Redbox for $32 million. And McDonald's even said they wouldn't take the $32 million. We could keep it for operating capital! In hindsight, turning our future over to what was at the time a somewhat dysfunctional company was a big mistake. Hindsight is always 20/20 and at the time it made sense.

I had dreamed the impossible dream and it had come true. Coinstar had a sales team that knew every store chain from Walmart to Kroger and beyond, even all over Canada, and they knew how to sell. So in a two-week period, we got them to agree to the 47 percent terms, plus they could also buy another 5 percent to be the majority owner for a fixed amount. Coinstar saved our ass and also gave us a great sales team. Bingo.

Now we had a machine that was working, we got funding longer-term, and we got the ability to place our machines where people actually wanted to rent movies. Grocery stores ended up being ideal because you typically go to a grocery store two and a half times per week, every two or three days. That's the perfect consistency and frequency with which to rent movies; you rent them and return them to the place you always shop. It becomes a part of your standard shopping routine. Easy.

It was a perfect deal. We had the funding to make these machines, which cost us anywhere from eight to twelve grand apiece. We were all set up. But once again, it was time for Tinkerbell.

For the next three years, we would install eight thousand machines a year, and we grew the business from $10 million or so to $1.5 billion. But while on that path, we hit two big obstacles. When our revenues got to about the $20 million mark, we started to see some people not coming back to use the machines. We went out and observed. We found a few small things, like in Phoenix the touchscreen was getting to be 130 degrees in the sun—we had to build a little curtain over it. But the biggest issue was that lines were forming. And people were giving up and abandoning the line. They would say, "I don't want to wait a couple minutes while I watch some guy browse through dozens of films." We installed second machines in some locations, but even with two machines, lines would still form.

The reason we went on to succeed was that we understood, when it came to a video vending machine, that one thing mattered more than anything else.

Transaction speed.

You may be familiar with the widely used measure of customer loyalty known as Net Promoter Score (NPS), which was invented by Fred Reichheld at Bain & Company. NPS is based on one question that you ask your customers: "How likely is it that you would recommend us to a friend or colleague?" The answers range from 0 (not at all likely) to 10 (extremely likely). To compute your NPS, you take the percentage of promoters (people who answer 9 or 10) and subtract the percentage of detractors (people who answer 0 to 6). NPS is supposed to predict the health of your business, because growth happens when you have lots of promoters and few detractors.

But while NPS may measure the health of your business and your likelihood to retain your customers, it doesn't tell you what to do to make it better. So we added a second question to our surveys: "What is the number one thing we could do to improve Redbox?" We learned after some starts and stops that the key wasn't trying to fix those things our detractors (who rated us a 0–6) wanted us to fix, such as fewer scratched DVDs, or what our promoters (who rated us a 9 or a 10) wanted us to do, which was add more copies of the big hits. Instead, we concentrated on the people who scored us 7 or 8 (the passively satisfied) on the original NPS question, because they were happy with us but could be happier and weren't raving about Redbox, nor were they trashing us like the detractors were. We got all sorts of answers, but the top answer was to make the transaction faster. Make the line shorter. Make the transaction speedier, make the movie selection easier.

The customers wanted fast. So we gave them fast.

Redbox machines were located where our existing and prospective customers shopped—in grocery stores and McDonald's—because that was where impulse purchases were most likely to take place. Impulse purchases have to be quick. If you had to fill out an application to get a Snickers bar at the supermarket checkout, they'd sell a lot fewer Snickers bars. Our attitude was similar—how quickly could we go from you realizing you'd like to rent a movie to your actually taking one home?

We observed that once there were seven or more people in line at the video machine, those after the first three or four would abandon the line and skip renting from Redbox. That matters, because half of the rentals took place between four p.m. and seven p.m. on Fridays and Saturdays. Every person who can't get their movie on Friday or Saturday night is a lost sale, lost revenue, a lost chance for us to make another buck from the machine and perhaps a customer who would not try us again.

So how do you make the transaction as fast as possible?

The first step was to reduce selection. This was counterintuitive. Our machines started with hundreds of titles and then up to six hundred DVDs. Most video stores had five thousand to ten thousand titles and dozens of copies each. Meanwhile Netflix and Blockbuster carried almost every title imaginable. This was a time when there was a huge trend to get exactly what you wanted, both the big hits and niche titles along the long tail, and as you could see when in the Starbucks order line, double macchiato, extra cream, don't stir, with a splash of chocolate was the trend.

Initially we tried to reflect the top movies released over a three-month period plus children's films and a fair amount of good B titles. Since seven to ten titles were released weekly, on average this added up to just under two hundred titles per quarter. When we observed browsers who scanned both the lightbox artwork and the titles on the touchscreen, we saw customers browsing for five or more minutes while others in line waited impatiently behind them. So our first change was to reduce titles in the lightbox down to sixty-six and limit the titles in the box. By reducing selection we brought the browse time down to a minute and a half.

The competing machines such as DVD Express and Blockbuster Express tried to replicate the video store experience. They couldn't stock ten thousand titles, but they could stock five hundred or even eight hundred titles. That meant people had to take time to browse. Browsers are thinking. People who are thinking aren't transacting. Lines get long and the business walks out the door. The competing machines failed. But that wasn't the only thing we did, nor was it the only reason we beat the shit out of our competitors.

Speed is also what caused us to price the rental at exactly one dollar a night. Early on we priced our rentals at 99 cents a night. Coming from Netflix and having video stores, I knew that we needed to do something that put more power of decision into the hands of customers. I knew that a big group of consumers were not comfortable with a monthly hit on their credit card as per

Netflix, and I also knew that many rental customers felt cheated when forced to pay and keep a movie for the three to five days in most rental programs. They also hated the huge cost of returning late or losing the movie, as Blockbuster would continue to charge $4 every few days until the cost reached as much as $200 for a single movie. We priced our program at one dollar a night up to twenty-four nights, and then the DVD was yours to keep. We found that 99 cents a night caused a bit of a calculation problem in our customers' eyes. We would ask them, "So if you keep this movie for four nights how much will you have paid?" They paused trying to calculate 99 cents times four days. Lo and behold, when we raised the price to one dollar a night, our customers got much more comfortable with that calculation, and that 1 percent increase led to a 4 percent rise in revenue.

The push for speed was also the reason that we didn't have memberships. We didn't need to know all about you the way that the Netflix site did, or the Blockbuster store did—speed meant you could walk up, pick a movie, and take it home, freeing up the kiosk for the next person. We even streamlined the credit approval process. In our first years using the Israeli one-ton machine, and even with our partner manufacturer DVDPlay, our software first required the customer to set up an account, then select the movie, and then, if already a member, to identify their account first. What a hassle. And even when we finally developed our own software and built our own kiosk, after the customer selected their DVDs our machine would first authorize and verify the customer's credit card, then instruct the robotics to go and get the DVDs and dispense them. By doing this serially we added 15–20 seconds on each transaction. We thought, "Well, how many credit cards failed?" Not many, a few percent. So by reducing the selection and processing the credit card without verifying it before dispensing the DVDs simultaneously, we cut a five-and-a-half-minute transaction down to a minute and three-quarters. We cut the time by two-thirds. Customers were delighted and our revenue grew dramatically per location from roughly $25,000 per year to an average of over $50,000 per year.

We also tried one innovation that didn't quite work. Why should the person *returning* a movie have to wait in line with the people renting? So we tested a machine with a second movie return slot on the side. It worked great in the lab. In the store, it meant the customer returning the movie had to squeeze right past the customer making a selection and approach the side of the machine. This resulted in a lot of dirty looks from movie renters whose personal space was invaded (and maybe they didn't want you to know why they, a fifty-year-old man, were renting *Happy Feet* yet again). We had to scrap the side return slot, because it creeped people out.

After we did all that testing and tinkering, the business just took off even further. We were doing fifty grand a machine, sixty grand a machine, seventy grand a machine every month. But with all the mass installation of the machines we were doing, we encountered another kind of problem altogether.

At this point, I and my team of vice presidents felt like we had hit a wall. Just like me, none of them had ever managed this size of business before. Some of them had teams of over a hundred people now. Their management shortcomings showed me where I, too, as the chief operating officer and bearing the newly added title of president, was personally failing. I had to wonder if Reed

Hastings had been right, that I didn't have what it took to be a senior executive in a big company.

As a manager, I had the philosophy that I needed to treat everybody the same; it didn't matter who you were or what level you were. I had to treat everybody the same with the same types of rewards, the same types of performance metrics, and so on. My approach, as well-meaning as it was, wasn't working at this level. I was losing people; people were losing their passion. They were burning out.

That's when Gregg Kaplan, who was still the CEO, said, "Listen, you need help. You need to learn better personnel management skills." He convinced me to hire Clyde Lowstuter, who is an organizational psychologist in Chicago and just an amazing guy. He's also a really, really sweet individual. He came in kind of like a psychiatrist. I mean, I'd literally sit on a couch in my office and talk to him.

He asked me: Why do I treat everybody the same? Why do I think that's going to work? Over the course of about nine months, he taught me a couple things. The big one was that everybody wants something different out of the job. The good news was, I cared enough about the people who work with me, and I wanted their lives to improve. That was why I thought I should treat everybody the same. But Clyde said, "No, if you really care about people, you've got to find out what's most important for *them*. Only then can you help them get what they want, not what you think they want. Some people want more freedom, some people want more money, some people want more vacation time, some people want more respect and others want to be challenged. Everybody wants something different." So I started this process of figuring out what was driving each person. I tried customizing their bonuses and rewards programs to fit in with what really mattered to them.

But even with that, I felt that we were hitting a wall. Instead of being innovative and introducing new products and services that could kick in, in the years to come we were just getting better and better at the processes we had built. The leaders were amazing. The process that Brian Rady ran that evaluated new location opportunities, taking only the cream of the crop and leaving what we determined were average-performing sites to our hungry competitor, Blockbuster Express, played a huge role in our ongoing success. Tim Hale's after-the-sale relationship building was instrumental in our location partners always renewing their contracts. Mary Leonard's field operations and customer service team installed one kiosk every hour, twenty-four hours a day, seven days a week, and operated them once installed and of course dealt with any technical or customer problems like a well-oiled machine. The tech team of Ratnakar Lavu and Eric Hoersten built a back end that was processing over two million transactions daily without any downtime or breaches, and the content team led by Scott Goldberg and then Mindy Herman exceeded all expectations for predicting demand. Their challenge was magnified by two facts. The first was that almost every new installation in one way or another cannibalized existing sites, and our customers were returning almost half of their DVD rentals to a different location from where they rented them. The dynamic duo of Mark Achler, who ran new business development, and

Gary Cohen, who ran marketing, ensured that we were considered a great company to rent from. Meanwhile Fred Stein, our general counsel, was like no other in that he not only guided us well but was also a major contributor to strategy. And Diane Pearse, who came to us from Crate & Barrel as our CFO, provided a deep understanding of how we measure the right kind of growth. One of the most rewarding actions I have taken in my career was to help Diane fulfill her dream of moving beyond finance into operations. She took over Mary Leonard's position as senior vice president of operations when we promoted Mary to the parent company. Diane's CFO position was filled by Galen Smith, who has run Redbox as CEO since 2016. It was an awesome team. One of the most difficult things I ever had to do as a manager was to regularly challenge and motivate this team of leaders. Their smarts and loyalty were beyond compare and I learned from them every day.

It was still about tinkering. When I finally learned how to motivate and incentivize each of our leaders, the revenue and introduction of innovative new services such as games and ticketing took off. The business doubled from around $300 million in annual revenue to $775 million and then in 2011 to $1.5 billion.

Tinkering optimizes raw product, technology, and people. You've got to create and fine-tune the right mix and caliber of people who can support each other, learn from each other, and have the passion to get better and smarter all the time. What I learned in this process ended up creating this team that just loved each other, worked hard for each other, and picked each other up when they were down.

Of course life isn't as easy as that, is it? Success itself creates problems. And our success brought us into conflict with the major studios in 2009, which was when lawsuits came rushing like a giant tsunami.

TAKEAWAY

Experiencing your product or service just like a customer is much more than a recommendation. And it is much more complicated than using the product. You need to shop for it, purchase it, receive it, use it, contact customer service, try to return it, explore the things that could perform better, smoother, and with less friction, and then prioritize plans for improving every aspect of your business. It is extremely important to demonstrate to your customers that you understand their issues and that you are methodically fixing things.

[7]

REDBOX OUTFOXES THE STUDIOS

Samma Sankappa (Right Thought)
We must bring others such as team or family and friends along
the same path we are following.

By July 2006, Redbox was primed for takeoff. We had overcome most of our challenges to growth. Redbox machines were renting DVDs to consumers in 1,350 locations, mostly McDonald's restaurants, and those kiosks had rented over eight million DVDs since 2003. We owned and manufactured our own robotic kiosk and the software that operated it, we had built a solid leadership team, and we'd even successfully met the challenge that McDonald's management had set for us, which was to find funding as a preface to spinning off or selling the company. Coinstar now owned 47 percent of Redbox with an option to purchase a further 4 or 5 percent by 2009.

Redbox focused mostly on hit movies, not a vast selection like a video store. Video stores required a special trip, while Redbox was something you did when you were going to the supermarket or McDonald's anyway. That meant our customers were walking by our machines several times a week—which generated frequent rentals just on impulse.

Coinstar had become a great partner. Their coin-counting machines were already in over fifteen thousand locations, including the fronts of many grocery store lobbies where a second machine from Redbox could do terrific business. Coinstar's reps were hungry to place that second machine in each store; we wanted to turn them loose. We were poised to start growing at what would become a blistering pace, installing Redbox machines at the rate of one per hour, every hour of every day, which we would reach in less than two years.

But while we were winning with consumers and expanding into a lot more retail locations, we still needed to do deals with the studios. We had to buy DVDs through a distributor, which slowed things down, increased costs, and limited our access to market development funds and co-op advertising programs. We were subject to credit checks and had to compete for supply with every video rental store in the country. It was time to be recognized as the big player we were about to become.

So we rented a suite at the Venetian in Las Vegas, the site of the VSDA convention, where all the video store chains and studios came to do business. By this time, video rental was an $8-billion-a-year business, rivaling the $9 billion from box office ticket sales. The studios came to Vegas to impress store chains like Blockbuster and Hollywood Video with their slate of upcoming movies and work out deals with them. And now we hoped they would want to make a deal with us.

The central feature of our suite was a large glass-top table, positioned in front of a huge flat-screen TV set. For each studio meeting, our senior leaders would array themselves around the room on cushy beige couches, waiting for the Hollywood bigwigs to arrive, buzzing with anticipation.

A few of the studios including Sony, which controlled Columbia Pictures and a huge chunk of all the hit movies about to be released, instead asked us to join them in their suite. Their suite had a large table with six or seven execs sitting around the table, and at the head was Marshall Forrester, their vice president of sales. We hadn't penetrated the Los Angeles market yet, so none of the studio execs had ever actually seen one of our kiosks. We showed off a video of our kiosk, then showed them our plans for nationwide growth along with videos of real customers using the kiosk. We demonstrated how easy it is for a consumer to use the Redbox kiosk. We showed them the rollouts we'd done in cities like Denver, Hartford, Salt Lake City, and Phoenix, with hundreds of machines per city.

Marshall, who's always been a bit of a stick in the mud, was hemming and hawing. Hrmm, hrmm, hrmm. The team turned to look at him. I knew that Sony generally liked to be a first mover on new ideas. They were the first to do a revenue-sharing deal with Netflix, a deal I'd helped initiate before we hired my friend and former distributor rep Ted Sarandos to take the lead on content. And now it was time for Sony to be the first to do a direct deal with a company that sold DVDs from a machine.

"Marshall," I said, "we want a direct deal with you, with Sony."

"Why?" Marshall harrumphed.

"We want to be in the same position that Blockbuster and Netflix are with you. We want Sony movies fast. We need to prep the DVDs, get the barcodes on them, and get them out to our teams and into the field—at the same time as Blockbuster and Netflix. And that's going to take a direct deal with Sony. So let's make it happen."

Just then Ben Feingold, Marshall's boss and the head of Sony's home video unit, made a theatrical entrance.

As you'll recall from Chapter 4, this wasn't my first time dealing with Ben. He'd insisted on packaging Sony's DVDs in the fragile, easily broken jewel cases when all the other studios had agreed on more reasonable plastic cases that fit on the store shelves. At that time, Ben was the impediment. He'd been wrong then. And now here he was, passing judgment on the future of Redbox.

Ben looked at me and all my staff arrayed around the room. He pressed his lips together into a flat line; his brows furrowed. "The worst mistake I ever made was doing a revenue-sharing deal with Netflix," he barked. "I am not going to do anything that will help Redbox to succeed."

The faces of my team immediately went from anticipation to dread.

He turned to each member of his team, sitting at the glass table. "Right?" he said to Marshall. Marshall grunted and nodded. "Right?" he said to the guy next to him. He nodded, too. This continued until everyone around the glass table had nodded. I knew a lot of these guys, and *they* knew that Redbox was likely to be one of the growing revenue streams of the future. But there was no way they would stand up to their big boss Ben Feingold after he'd thrown down the gauntlet. They weren't about to lose their jobs.

I sat silent for a minute, wanting to be careful of my response. I realized there was nothing we could accomplish here, so I said to all, "Well, I guess this meeting is over." And the Redbox team stood with me and we left. The conversation full of expletives as we walked back to the elevator reflected our disappointment and shock.

Before I tell you what happened with the studios after that meeting—and it wasn't all bad news—let's spend a minute on what had made Redbox successful up to that point. There was plenty of ingenuity. But it wasn't enough to be smart. It took a lot of intuition and data—and an attitude of constant testing and adjustment—to become the only kiosk video rental company that mattered. Competitors like Blockbuster had attempted to innovate with machines in places like the UK and Italy. Up to that point, all of them had failed.

In an ideal world, you figure out what the customer wants— or anticipate it—and they love you forever. Giving the customer what they want is a core principle of mine, and it's one reason why my companies are sometimes in conflict with the movie industry. The movie industry's job is to tell you what you want and then get you to pay for it over and over again (in the theater, in the rental store, on HBO, on cassette, then DVD, then Blu-Ray, and iTunes, and so on, and so on).

But sometimes it's not a question of giving the customer what they want, or telling the customer what they want. Sometimes it's just a question of what the company has to do to survive.

That's the situation we faced a few years later in 2009. Fred Stein, Redbox's general counsel, walked into my office one day. Fred was a good guy, a problem solver, but when he walked into your office, you knew you had a serious problem. And Fred showed me a lawsuit from a law firm that made big bucks filing class-action lawsuits on behalf of people in wheelchairs, based on the Americans with Disabilities Act (ADA). The ADA said that the controls on our machines needed to be no more than forty-eight inches off the ground, where a wheelchair user can reach them. Our screens were four inches too high. By this point we had over ten thousand kiosks, and this was a big problem.

Our leadership team met weekly, a practice I'd learned from Reed at Netflix. So I showed them the problem and asked for ideas on how to fix it. We already had a $5,000 bonus in place for people who came up with good ideas to improve the kiosk—now we had an urgent need for that sort of innovation.

We struggled for months trying to find an affordable solution. Retrofitting the machines and moving the screens down would be incredibly expensive. At one point we even considered digging holes under the machines and dropping them four inches into the ground or the floor, but that idea wouldn't fly with our retail partners—they agreed to a machine in their lobby, not a jackhammer going into their floor. Every solution looked expensive enough to bankrupt us.

Finally, as I was talking to one of the engineers about the problem, he said, "Hey, they can reach the bottom of the screen, right?"

"Sure," I said. "But some of the buttons they need to operate are at the top of the screen."

"Well, this is software. Let's move the buttons."

My mouth dropped open. This was a software fix and could even be done remotely at scale—my favorite kind of tweak. We engineered a button on the bottom of the screen that when selected put everything you needed to touch within reach of a person in a wheelchair. We ran it by the ADA experts—they said it would fly.

It was a software rollout; not a single machine needed to be taken apart or jackhammered further into the floor. It cost, basically, nothing.

There were other problems. Our machines needed to communicate to our servers so, among other things, we could verify people's credit cards. This meant that every machine had a cellular phone antenna on it. But in the late 2000s, cell communication was not completely dependable—sometimes the cell antenna would get knocked off the machine. So we designed the machines to operate in an offline mode until a technician could repair and reconnect it. This meant we had to trust the transaction until the connection was made again. And that meant that sometimes we'd get taken by fraudulent transactions.

We downloaded a list of the most common fraudulent customers to all the machines, but of course we missed some. A common scam looked like this: Somebody rents a movie or a videogame with a Visa gift card that can be purchased at almost any grocery store. The fraudster uses the card to rent from Redbox, as we never required more than a valid credit card. Then they never return the DVDs and, usually, a high-cost PlayStation 2 game. We don't have their name or contact info, so we can't bill them or charge them since there was no balance left on the gift/debit card. And Visa and MasterCard wouldn't allow us to identify or treat gift cards differently from other credit cards. So the next question was: How do we get out from under the fraud?

After hiring former Visa execs as advisors, our team of analysts and I devised a credit scoring system that would estimate the likelihood of fraud and attempt to not complete a transaction with those customers. The fraud score for each transaction would allocate points based on how much your transaction looked like the ones most likely to be fraudulent. Horror movie renters were twice as likely to be fraudsters. People who rented between midnight and six a.m., three times as likely. So if you rented a horror movie at two a.m., you might get the message "unable to complete transaction"—because you looked just like a rip-off artist. This algorithm by 2011 was saving us over $60 million annually.

The studios like Sony weren't the only big partners we had to deal with. Every Redbox kiosk was in a retail location. And every retailer had its own biases. We had to be very good partners, because while a Redbox machine might generate $5,000 to $10,000 a year in partner fees for the retailer who hosted it, the last thing that retailer wants is for anything to interfere with the rest of its business.

Take McDonald's. While at that point the parent company still owned a huge hunk of Redbox, it was up to the individual franchisees in a given area to determine if they'd host Redbox machines inside or just outside their restaurants. We had data showing that a McDonald's with a Redbox kiosk generated 4 percent greater revenues from food service, because the kiosk creates a reason to come back to the restaurant—to return the disk. The 4 percent boost was significant to a restaurant that would generate between $1.5 million and $2.5 million per year.

But money isn't everything to a restaurant owner. We had pretty close to saturated Salt Lake City, with one kiosk for every 2,500 residents. On some street corners, there were three machines: one in a McDonald's, one in a gas station, and one in a grocery store. But when we tried to expand to nearby Provo, the franchise owners had one condition: no racy films. They were very clear that McDonald's is a family place; as one explained, invoking the hallowed name of McDonald's founder, "If Ray Kroc knew we were renting R-rated movies at McDonald's, he'd be rolling over in his grave." So we agreed: no R-rated titles in Provo.

To be sure, there was a loophole. To make things convenient, we allowed customers to return DVDs to any machine, regardless of where they rented them. People were renting R-rated films near their workplaces in Salt Lake City, then returning them near their homes in Provo. So while there were no glowing ads for racy movies in Provo, those disks were in the machines, and you could see them on the menus. And damned if the people in Provo weren't happy to rent titles full of nudity and curse words, regardless of the opinions of the people who owned the local McDonald's franchises.

Of course, the challenges with McDonald's franchises were nothing compared to working with the biggest retailer on the planet: Walmart.

Of every $9 spent in retail in America, one dollar goes to Wal-Mart. With nearly five thousand locations in the United States, Walmart attracts 95 percent of consumers to shop there in any given year; 275 million people shop there every three months. Walmart is the eight-hundred-pound gorilla of retail—a must-have partner that drives a hard bargain, not just for partners like Redbox but for every company it deals with.

We were hot to be in Walmart stores. And we had a foothold; by 2009 we had around 660 Redbox kiosks in Walmart stores. We were a good partner, too. We could show that people stopping by on an unplanned visit to rent or return movies were typically buying $35 worth of other stuff in Walmart during that visit.

But we were at their mercy—and in many cases they were merciless. In 2008, when our partnership was growing, there was a new guy in charge of "store presentation." One day he called my team and me down to Walmart headquarters in Bentonville, Arkansas. (Anyone who's ever worked with Walmart knows—when Walmart calls you to Bentonville, you go to Bentonville.) When we arrived, he took us to their prototype store of the future in nearby Rogers, Arkansas. And there, he revealed his new concept for the real estate just as you enter the store—the space where the claw machine, the Coke machine, and the Redbox machine live. He turned to us and said, "Hey, what do you see that is different here?"

What we saw is that everything—the Redbox kiosk excluded—was a beautiful shade of Walmart blue. "I want color coordination," he said. And if you wanted to stay at Walmart, Redbox was going to be in a blue box. "But it's called *Red*box," I pleaded. "Doesn't matter," he said. I looked around and realized the Coca-Cola machine was now a Pepsi blue. Noticing my gaze, the Walmart exec looked straight at me and said, "If I can make Coca-Cola change their color to Walmart blue, by God Redbox will do it too."

In my head I started to calculate how much this would cost: several thousand dollars per machine. Removing the red kiosk, installing a newly manufactured blue one, and then reinstalling the old one somewhere else. But like all good Walmart partners we gritted our teeth and painted around two thousand Redbox kiosks Walmart blue. To my surprise we actually saw an uplift in sales of around 1 percent. But then he was let go and all new Redbox installs went back to red again.

That wasn't the last hiccup with Walmart. It turned out that Walmart designates a person from one of the movie studios to be a "category captain" who analyzes and determines buying for DVDs across all the stores. (It's a rotating position; a different studio was in charge of it every couple of years.) At one point, one of these category captains (from Warner) figured out that Walmart was selling $5 billion worth of DVDs and that rentals from Redbox could be putting a dent in that. They surveyed people renting movies at Redbox kiosks in Walmart stores and asked, "Would you have considered buying that movie if it wasn't available for rent at Redbox for just one dollar a night?" About 8 percent said they would have considered purchasing the movie. And the studios extrapolated that to estimate that they were losing $400 million in sales because of the Redbox kiosks.

But it's easy to imagine you'd pay $16 for a movie that you'd watch only once, if somebody asks you when you're holding the disk in your hand. That's not necessarily how it works in the real world. And every one of those Redbox kiosks was generating $5,000 to $10,000 in profits for the stores—not to mention the sales of other stuff from people who pop into Walmart to return a movie. Within a month or two we were back in Bentonville meeting with execs from both Walmart and Anderson Distributing, a company that grew quite big based on its core Walmart business, and one of the several topics was "When are we going to change out our high-energy-use lightboxes for LED boxes?" as well as addressing the continued challenge by the studio partners of Walmart that Redbox is costing DVD sales.

At this meeting were perhaps a dozen execs including the Redbox team. My job as president was to kick off the meeting and try to ensure that we did not get kicked out of Walmart. It was an early-morning meeting and we had been out late the night before. I asked one of my team to pull up my PowerPoint slides on the monitor when suddenly I realized not only was this the wrong presentation, but the second and third slides of the slide-show would probably upset the Walmart attendees and risk our deal with them.

I was panicking and while only a few seconds passed while I sipped some coffee, it seemed like an eternity. How do I get out of making this presentation? What do I do? Without thinking about it I grabbed my chest and did my best to fake a heart attack or something serious enough to warrant a rescheduling. Our vice president of client relations, Tim Hale, helped me up and took me to the bathroom, where I stayed long enough to hear that the meeting would be rescheduled.

Eventually, after a lot of concern that we'd get kicked out, the guys in charge of the real estate at the front of the store told the DVD sales guys to stuff it, and we stayed right where we belonged. With Redbox kiosks that were actually *red*, of course.

But as it turned out, this was just a harbinger of more trouble to come with the studios.

As you may have gathered from what you've read so far, Sony's rejection of Redbox in 2006 hardly even slowed us down. In the four years that passed after Ben Feingold gave us the finger in that suite at the Venetian, Redbox became a very big deal.

By 2008 Redbox had gotten to $175 million in revenue. My team would then double revenue again, to $355 million the next year, and double it again to $775 million the following year. Then incredibly we doubled again to $1.5 billion the following year. In 2011, we did $1.5 billion in revenue and had $325 million in free cash flow. That was a source of pride for me, but there were plenty of obstacles to overcome along the way.

For example, in 2009, Warner, Universal, Fox, and Paramount supplied us with DVDs on the same schedule as the ones they shipped to video stores, based on the very deals we started to negotiate in Vegas back in 2006. Ben was gone from Sony—and we had a deal with them too. Only Disney was missing, and they would soon be doing a direct-supply deal with us as well.

In fact, we were now closing in on being the number three video rental player in the nation, behind Blockbuster and Hollywood Video, but ahead of Movie Gallery. And Blockbuster, a billion dollars in debt, was on the verge of bankruptcy.

Having a big, rapidly growing rental player charging only a dollar a night made the studios nervous. So we believed they hatched a scheme to put us in our place. We would often hear that our one-dollar-a-night charge "demeaned" the film they had invested perhaps tens of millions of dollars in producing.

To understand how the studios' scheme worked, you need to understand something fundamental about the movie business. It operates on the concept of "windows" for different releases at different time periods. The objective is to maximize revenue from each window without significantly cannibalizing subsequent windows. First, a movie appears in movie theaters along with an advertising campaign. A few months later, it gets released to hotel movie rentals and airplanes. Months after that, the DVD comes out and you can buy or rent it at Blockbuster or Redbox, or other retail outlets where DVDs are sold. Perhaps a year after the original release, it appears on a pay TV service like HBO or Showtime.

And then, after enough years pass, it's licensed to appear on traditional TV channels like USA, TNT, or ABC.

This windowing system is designed to maximize revenue. It squeezes every last dollar out of one channel before making the movie available on another channel. If the movie was on HBO at the same time it appeared in the theater, fewer people would buy tickets. If it was for rent at Blockbuster at the same time as you could see it on TNT, there would be less money generated at Blockbuster. And the important factor is that the studio could collect $1.50 to $2 of every Blockbuster rental as compared to 15 to 25 cents on a viewing on cable. Keeping the windows spaced out and separate is a fundamental guiding principle for the studios.

They all buy into it in a compatible way to create a nice, simple, well-defined set of negotiations with their various distribution channels. All this money then flows into the studios, and they use it to pay the producers, directors, stars, and other collaborators who created the movies in the first place. It is literally written into every contract in the movie business.

Every new channel must fit into this framework. That's how the distribution of movies to video on demand (VOD) and streaming ended up being negotiated—the studios had to figure out where those channels belong in the window structure (eventually, parallel with video rentals).

With this in mind, you can understand what three studios tried to do to us in the summer of 2010: to move Redbox, along with Netflix, into a new window, *behind* the movie rental places like Blockbuster and Hollywood Video. Fox, Universal, and Warner—representing about 40 to 45 percent of the movie business—told us we'd have to wait four to six weeks after the movie goes on sale at

Walmart and for rental at Blockbuster (and for rent at all the video stores) before we could put it in our machines. The purpose of this move was to give people a chance to pay a higher rental fee or to buy movies from these stores before they became available for rental at Netflix and Redbox.

You'd imagine that Reed Hastings at Netflix would have a fit at being disrespected like this. But he was fine with it because Netflix customers were less interested in seeing the big hits the first week of release. But *I* wasn't fine with it. So we began to negotiate.

The studios asked us to charge $4 for four nights instead of a dollar a night. What I tried to explain to the often deaf ears of the studio execs was that $1 a night is the same as $4 for four nights and that because of our pricing, people were renting movies they wouldn't rent at a $4 price point. And as a result, our disks were constantly in circulation and not sitting on the shelves as they did at a Blockbuster store. Customers didn't want to keep them for four nights and pay four times as much. So that was a nonstarter.

They also wanted to sell us disks at $5 to $8 a disk instead of $16 and then take a big percentage of our revenue, and they wanted us to destroy the disks once we were done with them instead of selling them used. (Studios hate used DVD sales, since they inhibit $15 consumer purchases of new DVDs and the studios get nothing from them.)

So I assembled my leadership team and we reviewed our options. We determined that while Fox and the other studios could refuse to sell direct to us until a title is in the new Redbox/Netflix rental window, they *couldn't* stop us from buying the title some other way. And according to a legal principle known as the first sale doctrine, we were allowed to rent any DVD that we purchased legally, regardless of how we purchased it. My senior vice president of operations, Mary Leonard, pointed out that we had eight hundred field employees who were conveniently located close to every single Redbox kiosk—and that those employees were also close to stores like Walmart, Best Buy, and Costco, where the DVDs we need would be on sale as soon as the studios release them, weeks *before* our delayed window would open.

Thus began one of the strangest guerrilla operations ever conceived.

Mary organized the field employees and gave them a new job: buy DVDs. We sent each employee a credit card. We told them how many we needed of each new title coming out from Fox, Universal, and Warner. And we turned them loose.

Soon our people were going into Walmart stores (which they were visiting anyway to service Redbox machines), Best Buy stores, and Costco stores and buying dozens or even hundreds of copies of just-released DVDs. *Date Night* was a Fox title, a comedy starring Tina Fey and Steve Carell, released on DVD on Tuesday, August 10, 2010 (DVDs nearly always first appear on Tuesday). Our employees went to Walmart or Best Buy or Costco on that Tuesday, piled fifty copies into a shopping cart, and then paid with the credit card we sent. Then they took the disks back to our warehouse, removed them from the packaging, applied a barcode, and got them ready to install in all the local Redbox machines by Wednesday or Thursday.

Sure, it cost a little more, but we had people with credit cards buying DVDs everywhere we needed them, and they were ready within days of when they went on sale, not weeks later. In fact, on a weekly basis we were buying at retail well over a hundred thousand copies of a single title. I remember saying to my team that unfortunately we are helping prove the studios' theory that if they stop providing rental inventory to Redbox, retail sales would increase. But those increased sales were from us, not real customers. They actually ended up costing a few bucks less than what we paid the studios for direct purchases, due to Walmart and others giving huge discounts in the first week of sales to draw consumers.

It got to the point where some of the store managers were just putting boxes of DVDs aside for us on the loading dock, because why go through the hassle of scanning them at the checkout counter?

There were a few problems with this plan.

We actually needed 300,000 copies of some of the big hit titles, and the most we could buy—and this was cleaning out almost all the national inventory in these major retailers—was around 125,000 copies. So we were short on those titles for a little while. And it was labor intensive to buy all those copies and remove the packaging. However, the demand was so great that our profit on these titles exceeded all others.

We had a few inevitable cases of credit card fraud—rogue Redbox employees buying refrigerators and washing machines instead of DVDs. One guy bought tens of thousands of dollars' worth of goodies like washing machines, clothes, and other stuff. We found these few people and fired them. No big deal.

Our Redbox employees got caught performing this guerrilla content acquisition tactic, of course. Craig Kornblau, president of Universal Pictures, took a photo of one of our guys sweeping a huge display of DVDs directly into a shopping cart—while wearing a bright red Redbox polo shirt. (They weren't supposed to wear the shirt—that was a mistake.)

At that point it became a war between us and the three studios. The other three studios—Disney, Paramount, and Sony—remained above the fray and were happy to keep sending us DVDs on the original release date while they waited to see how this feud ended. But Fox, Universal, and Warner started to get a bit nasty in my opinion. They started advertising DVDs with copy that said *Get it now: Not available at Netflix or Redbox.*

The studios in the feud with us started restricting how many copies they'd sell to places like Best Buy and Walmart. And then the stores put limits on the number of copies any one person can buy, because they didn't want disappointed consumers complaining. Our little scheme began to falter.

We went back to the negotiating table. They knew what we'd been doing, and they also knew we needed more disks. So we came to an agreement. They reduced the delay on our window to four weeks. They cut the cost we paid for DVDs to less than half. And we agreed to share revenue and destroy the DVDs once the demand ebbed.

As it turns out, only 10 percent of customers really wanted the disk as soon as it was available. The rest saw it show up at Redbox and rented it then.

The company came out of this little spat doing fine. But I didn't.

Pleasing customers and partners is hard. But pleasing the board can be harder.

Growth is the drug that all businesses need. If you stop growing, you become just another competitor in a crowded market.

As I'd learned at Netflix and put into action at Redbox, that growth comes from many sources. Tweaking the offering based on what you learn about customers creates growth. Making and expanding strong partnerships—like the ones we had with retailers—is essential to growth. And of course, you need to continue to have solid relationships with your suppliers—in our case, the movie studios—to grow, because without product, you have nothing.

But I had my sights on something bigger. Growth from the day-to-day improvements was *tactical*. That is, it came from fighting the fight a little better every day. But along with tactical excellence, you need *strategic* vision—the ability to look out beyond the horizon. To me, even in 2010, it was clear that the business of renting physical disks would eventually peter out. Internet-connected TV sets were becoming a reality, and companies like Apple and TiVo were creating boxes that let you see internet content on your TV screen. It was just a matter of time before movies started streaming to your TV, too.

As you read this, you may think, wasn't it obvious that streaming was the future? I congratulate you on your 20/20 hindsight. In 2010, it was far from obvious—and the timing was tricky. Netflix and Hulu had created streaming services, but they didn't have much in the way of recent movies. It was clear to me that, for strategic reasons, Redbox needed to get into streaming, too. So even as I was negotiating with the movie studios and the likes of Walmart, I was trying to get a Redbox streaming service off the ground.

We had fifty million regular users that we could channel into a streaming service. I planned to give the streaming service free to people who committed to rent five DVDs at $4.99 a month. What

I needed was content. Content is expensive. So I told the Coinstar board of directors we needed $500 million to fund it.

But the board was becoming frustrated.

Earlier in the year—before Fox, Universal, and Warner decided to go to war on our rental window—I'd forecast $318 million in gross revenue for the fourth quarter of 2010. But that number didn't contemplate sending employees shopping for DVDs and failing to get quite enough to maximize revenue. It didn't contemplate studios placing ads that said *Not available at Netflix and Redbox*. It didn't contemplate my need to make a deal that delayed our DVD availability until twenty-eight days after the release date on more than 40 percent of new DVDs in the machines. In the end, we had a shortfall. Revenue for the fourth quarter came in at $302 million, $16 million below the forecast, or 95 percent of what I'd promised. My target was not to be off by more than 3 percent.

That was enough to make the board lose some faith in me. Coinstar execs weren't about to pony up half a billion dollars on my strategic vision. "You want streaming? Find a partner to fund it," they told me.

So even as I was negotiating deals with the contentious studios, I was seeking out partners with deep pockets for a streaming venture. I found two pretty good prospects: Verizon, which wanted to get deeper into content, and Charlie Ergen's Dish Network.

Dish Network was an interesting company. It was one of the most idiosyncratic players in the TV business. Charlie Ergen started it by driving his truck around servicing those huge satellite dishes you used to see in rural areas. Eventually after many years of hard work he launched his own satellites and started his own service, building it up to be the number two satellite player in the United States, behind DirecTV. While DirecTV was bought and sold to different players, Dish Network wasn't—because Ergen wanted to control everything himself. I had heard that he was temperamental but focused and of course a very successful micromanager—and he was super frugal, as I had also heard that he required his staff when traveling on business to share hotel rooms to save money. But he also made audacious deals. He bought Sling Media, for example, a company that made streaming set-top boxes similar to Apple TVs. I knew he had the stones to make a deal with us and could pull the trigger as soon as the terms were what he wanted.

After months of negotiation, my business development team and I made a deal with him. He insisted on control, owning 51 percent of our streaming venture, but it would have the Redbox name on it. He was convinced that many of the content rights he'd negotiated for Dish Network, rights for which I believed he paid over $5 billion a year, would enable him to stream videos using the internet. It was a grueling negotiation, but we came to terms. On Wednesday night, April 6, 2011, I flew back from Dish Network's offices in Colorado to our headquarters in Chicago and knew our deal was close to being done.

When I opened my PC on the following morning, I saw some news that made me spit out my coffee: Dish Network had bought Blockbuster out of bankruptcy. I felt like I had been played—Redbox was just the backup plan. Our negotiation was moot—there was no longer a deal on the table.

What about Verizon? Its dealmakers insisted that the company never lose money on a single customer from day one. That was no way to compete with the now-growing Netflix streaming service. (Think about all the big start-ups that have succeeded in the last twenty years, from Amazon to Twitter; most of them lost money at the start. When you're seeking rapid growth and acquiring users or subscribers, you can't insist on profitability from day one.) Because of Verizon's terms, we'd have to cover the cost of content for every customer with the subscription fee. That would choke off the growth and doom the service. But at this point we had no choice. We had to go with what we knew would be a deal that was unlikely to catch on. Verizon was our new streaming partner.

Unfortunately, that meant that the writing was on the wall for me as well. While I'd succeeded in growing Redbox into a billion-dollar business with over thirty-five thousand locations, I'd missed the fourth-quarter revenue estimates and struck out on the streaming deal with Dish Network. The board gave up on me. Redbox's founder Gregg Kaplan, who at that point was the CEO of our parent company Coinstar, said I'd need to step down.

The zen disruptor had disrupted the video rental business once again with perseverance, close attention to data, and scrappy dealmaking. It was too bad I didn't get to launch the streaming venture with the iconic Charlie Ergen, who I suspect is very unhappy with the money he spent on Blockbuster. But this wasn't the end for me. I still had one more very big chance to turn the movie business upside down.

Despite leaving the company, I had proven a lot to myself. I'd shown that I could manage and grow a big company. I had shown that the tinkering method, which is central to the zen disruptor's approach, could eventually solve any problem.

But while I was a success in business, my family life and my philosophical core weren't as solid as they should have been. So I took a break for a while and worked on discovering who I really was.

--- **TAKEAWAY** ---

Learning how to scale and not grow too fast is a completely new skill. I have found that using some of the early piecemeal manufacturing processes developed at Ford Motors in the early twentieth century can be very helpful. Break the task into units that are clear and understandable. For Redbox the unit was a group of around 150 kiosks within a fairly small driving region. Each unit had a manager, three technicians, and five merchandisers. That was roughly the most efficient grouping, so sales targeted a local partner such as a regional grocer, Walgreens, and so on, that fit those numbers; then we went to work building the kiosks, getting the install details approved, installing the kiosks, and beginning operations. Developing a sales qualification process in order to take the best opportunities first set us apart from National Cash Register and Blockbuster, who went on a land grab, which eventually dragged them down.

[8]

THE INTERREGNUM

Samma Sati (Right Mindfulness)
We must sort through all the baggage we have picked up
through our lives and put it away in the right compartment;
this allows us to understand what is important and what is not
and to resolve open issues in our conscious and subconscious.

So once again I had been let go from a company I'd helped to
become successful. Unlike when I was gracefully transitioned
to being a consultant at Netflix, this time I did not have to be
too concerned about money. It was really the first time in my life
I came to appreciate the liberating impact of that feeling. Like
most people, I had always lived month-to-month or day-to-day.
Fortunately, I had always been quite frugal and had continued to
save and pay bills on time. Now that I was financially secure, it
changed the way I woke up in the morning and the way I evaluated opportunities.

In the last two chapters, I didn't write too much about my
relationship with my family. The truth was that I had been con-
sumed with work and had worked almost every day, including

Christmas and New Year's. My wife had concentrated on running the house and making it an amazing place to live, and for our children to grow up. I was spending most of the time in Chicago, where Redbox was headquartered, while she was running things at our home in Mill Valley. I was home only six to eight days a month, and even then my interactions with my family were pretty superficial. During that time, my kids Joaquin, Emiliano, and Paloma had basically grown up and were off to college.

But now that I'd left Netflix and was in solid financial shape, there was an incredible reduction in that hungry passion I had for making money. I was almost sixty years old. My kids' education was all paid for, I owned three homes free and clear of any mortgages, and we had plenty of savings and investments. Still, something was nagging me. But I decided not to face that issue and instead launched into my first real extended vacation, ever.

This was going to be a trip throughout Southeast Asia with Zamora. It was like the first-class version of my teenage adventure in Europe. But once again, I had no firm plan. We decided each week where to go next, usually for about a week, and let the weather dictate the place. We started in Hong Kong, then went to Hanoi, Bangkok, Chiang Mai, and the Thai islands of Phi Phi; Yangon and Bagan in Burma (now known as Myanmar); Laos; and then Siem Riep, Cambodia, and Kuala Lumpur in Malaysia. That was the first month and a half.

At first it was liberating to spend a little time relaxing. The Southeast Asia trip was a way to see if I could be happy just lying by the pool. But I hated it. I kept thinking, "Oh, fuck, what am I doing."

Next we went to India to deepen our spiritual connections beginning with ten days at the Vipassana Meditation Center outside

Jaipur. I had often meditated but never to the extent I was about to embark upon. The center was about an hour's drive from Jaipur, surrounded by dry rustic villages. Entering the compound, we found a lush complex filled with a variety of wild animals. Monkeys and peacocks were everywhere sounding off, and thousands of birds were circling above. The birds kept landing in various trees in the complex, and I felt as if this was a sign of the peacefulness and importance of this place.

When we checked in there were about eight others there, mostly young, rugged backpackers from France, Germany, and the Czech Republic. Two other Americans arrived, and the remaining people were Indian. The ten-day retreat was primarily for meditation novices unready for the skill required for ten hours a day of meditation but looking to embrace it.

At check-in we surrendered our electronics, books, writing materials, food, and all connections to the outer world except a few clothes and bathroom items. We were then separated into male and female sides of the complex and each shown to a small individual concrete cell. Mine had a small wooden bed on one side with a sink with cold water, and a separate little room with a toilet that really was just a hole with a bucket you could use to flush it. We were told that there would be no talking or communicating with anyone over the next ten days, with one exception: you could ask the teacher a question during the daily lesson. This I knew would be my biggest challenge, as I love to talk and ask for opinions.

The morning schedule each day went like this: Wake up to a loud gong at four a.m. each morning. Wash briefly. Communal vegan breakfast at 4:30 a.m. A little walking or return to your cell.

At 5:30 a.m., a group ninety-minute meditation in a large temple, with the women on the opposite side from the men. It was cold so we would often be wrapped in blankets and sit on a pillow or two in the lotus position.

We first learned the Anapana exercise of concentrating on the feel of the air coming out of your nostrils sweeping over the upper lip. There was no chanting, we were just focusing on the feel. As we progressed, we began the full Vipassana exercise of closing your eyes and imagining you can feel the crown of your head and slowly progressing down your body to your toes and then back again. I kept imagining the scene in the 1920s German silent film *Metropolis*, seeing the electric rings go up and down around the body of the robot.

Vipassana is a form of Buddhism practiced primarily in Myanmar and Sri Lanka with retreats all over the world. The major thesis of Vipassana is that the only things you know for sure are those that you feel or see firsthand. The Vipassanas also believe that all emotions including anxiety, happiness, and sadness begin with a physical sensation and that if you can neutralize the connection between the sensation and your brain, you can control the emotional reactions. In the meditation practice of feeling every inch of your skin and body as you pass from head to toe, you observe any bodily feelings and in your mind say something like, "Oh my stomach is hurting, interesting," and move on to the next part of your body. You are simply observing the stomachache and not reacting. By doing so over time you reach a profound sense of peace, focus, and control.

Our early group meditation ended with a thirty-minute lecture from a teacher. Then we exited, heads bowed so as not to look at anyone in the eyes. There was a short break, followed by another hour of meditation on your own. Next, another short break of walking among the screaming peacocks and rambunctious tree monkeys. Then another hour of meditation back in the temple.

Next came a communal vegan lunch. You grabbed a plate, walked down a line of volunteer servers, drank lemon water, sat and ate quietly, and took another walk followed by more meditation. By eight p.m. you would have meditated ten hours. We did that every day.

By the third day, as the loneliness of noble silence kicked in, I found a number of voices taking turns speaking in my mind. Soon they were taking up different positions against each other and arguing. The first big argument was "Why the fuck am I here? I should get out of here back to civilization." That would be countered by "Well, you started it, now finish, it might be good for you." Then a third voice said, "You weak and ungrateful chump, what a loser." This would go on for hours, and during meditation I would battle inside my brain to quiet these arguments. I recalled the person who checked us in saying that they do not let novices leave before the full ten days because if you leave in the middle of the program, the internal strife caused by these voices can cause you to suffer long term.

After the fourth day, as I would walk, head bowed in silence, among the trees watching the feet and legs of others passing by, I started to see some of the younger Indian guys quietly kicking rocks to each other in kind of a pickup soccer game. By the fifth day I was tearing up pieces of toilet paper and creating a checkerboard on the floor of my cell. The lengths the brain goes to not be alone with itself are like a drug addict searching for that next hit.

Upon reaching the eighth day, a sense of peace and contentment and confidence overcame me and has stayed with me ever since, although from time to time the intensity has varied. I realized that the strong and powerful voices that had scared me so much were all parts of me, like friends I could count on—they were helping and supporting each other in their own ways, and supporting me as well.

Like most novices who get through the full ten nights and eleven days, the first thing you do upon returning to civilization is talk and eat. We checked into a hotel in Jaipur that had been a palace in the 1930s. In the bathroom was a digital scale. To my surprise, I had lost twenty pounds without knowing it by eating vegan and meditating, even though there was no physical activity other than short calm walks.

The lessons from that trip have lasted for the rest of my life. I realized that as humans, we put up all sorts of walls and obstacles to thinking sincerely about our lives and ourselves. There is a protective mechanism in your brain that kicks in when you try to think about such things, and it is telling you, "Don't worry about this now, you can deal with it another time." It took eight days of meditation for me to deal with my crap instead of avoiding it. It takes an experience like I had in Jaipur to focus your mind on what really matters in your life.

I started to realize that my initial fascination with Buddhist thought, from back when I was a teenager, was leading me in the right direction. A lot of knowledge and experience has been developed in Buddhism to help you as an individual to find your own path to happiness. Meditation is part of that path. And one reason that Buddhism syncs with me is that it states that regardless of what anyone else does, you are responsible for finding your own happiness.

From my perspective, even with everything I have done, it feels as if the most important thing in life is to have children, and second is to enjoy the passage of the very short time we have to be alive. That enjoyment comes from being a good person and helping other people, which gives you meaning. That may seem trite, but living it is not something that comes naturally without effort.

What followed over the next three months after Jaipur was a journey that took us to southern India, then Sri Lanka, over to the Maldives, to Java and Bali, then back to Hong Kong, and finally, home again. While I had a great renewal in my practice of meditation, I soon had a huge sense of "not belonging" and not being needed anywhere. My life had lost some of its meaning, at least as far as work was concerned. I don't think there had ever been a time in my life that I did not have a plan or project that I was working on. This was hard to deal with and brought with it a fear of the future that I could not get a grip on, nor could I control where it took my mind during the day.

I had to somehow break out of this funk, so I began to think about becoming involved with more early-stage companies.

I started calling a few of my colleagues from Redbox. One, a former software engineer who had been key in Redbox's streaming partnership with Verizon, introduced me to Tony Conrad, a partner at True Ventures. Tony was a new kind of person for me: smart and a true Silicon Valley multimillion-dollar success story. His fund is famous for having invested early in Fitbit and for also selling a couple of companies to AOL.

Tony took me to a new coffee start-up in San Francisco called Blue Bottle Coffee, which his technology venture capital firm had invested in. That seemed strange. He described the venture as a retail coffee experience, and he wanted me to see it in order to understand how important the treatment of the customer was. Amid all the competition on Market Street, this little coffee shop had a line of thirty people waiting. Once we got in, I saw why. The shop had five specialty workers all dedicated to making one cup of coffee: one ground the beans, the second put the coffee in the machine and tamped it down, the third person ran the machine to output the coffee, the fourth person poured it and then mixed the cream or the milk, and then the last person handed it to you and handled the payment.

In the end, you had also witnessed this beautiful, collaborative experience. At Blue Bottle, every single detail related to making the coffee was perfect, with the right temperature and exact amounts all being measured with tremendous attention to detail. Overall, the taste and the quality of the beverage met every expectation for the best coffee possible.

We sat down and Tony explained that his firm's philosophy revolved around investing in companies where the customer is number one and, within the service provided, the customer gets to watch a brand going all out in order to create this wonderful, live, and unusual experience.

A few years later, Nestlé bought a majority stake in Blue Bottle for a reported half billion dollars.

Tony also introduced me to the young founder of Quarterly, a company that True had invested in. Quarterly was a subscription box company that was sent out, yes, quarterly, with each box designed by high-profile influencers who fans wanted to connect with. There was the author Tim Ferris, who wrote *The 4-Hour Workweek*; Bill Nye the Science Guy; Alexis Ohanian, the founder of Reddit; Nina Garcia, the famous fashion journalist; and a dozen or so others just as high profile. Their boxes cost anywhere from $90 to as much as $5,000 for Tim Ferris's super box.

Tony asked me to meet the founder of Quarterly, Zach Frechette, and, ideally, "teach him how to be a CEO." I took the project provided I could hire my youngest son and recent University of Colorado graduate Emiliano. While at first I was energetic and passionate about my teacher-advisor role, I soon found joy only in the two or three days a week that I would share an apartment with Emiliano off Santa Monica Boulevard in West Hollywood.

Meanwhile, another former Redbox regional supervisor had reached out and introduced me to a colorful character who was running a medical marijuana kiosk company. What a crazy story that company turned out to be. By doing a reverse merger into a penny stock and tapping growing investor interest in anything to do with the marijuana business that could be accessed in the public market, the founder was able to ride the company's value up to an unbelievable $900 million. My former Redbox colleague was working for this company because of his kiosk experience. When the founder told my former colleague that he wanted to build a board of directors of solid reputable businesspeople as a step toward moving his penny stock to NASDAQ, where he knew valuations could go even higher, my friend suggested he talk to me.

The guy clearly was a super smart and passionate businessperson. He immediately pointed out that he had broken some business rules in the past but had paid his dues and learned those lessons and wanted his company to be run properly. He was building a board that very soon included, along with me, Ned Siegel, the George W. Bush–appointed former ambassador to the Bahamas, and Jennifer Love, a former assistant director of the FBI and now the head of security at a major cruise line.

In hindsight, the clear sign that this would end badly was how overly generous he was in paying us board members with stock options. Our relationship with the company started in April 2013, and by October he was asking us as board members to sign off on three years of financials to submit to NASDAQ for listing there. Well, thank God for Ned and Jennifer, as they demanded that before we sign anything, we have an unaffiliated accountant review the financials. Within a week we were advised not to sign, as irregularities were found, especially concerning the way the company recognized revenue. It seemed that his sales guys would sign multiyear service contracts to provide marijuana-dispensing kiosks but recognize the full two-year revenue in the month the deal was signed. This tended to overstate revenue and potentially played a role in the crazy high stock price.

The company had meager actual revenues yet was valued at tens and even hundreds of millions of dollars. Since it was a public company, now that we as the board had doubts about the veracity of numbers that shareholders and investors had relied on in previous financial statements, we were advised that we needed to publicly disclose that the board was not going to sign off on the financials. That news cratered the stock and as a result generated a flood of lawsuits against the company and even against us as board members.

What followed was three years of lawsuits and almost bi-weekly meetings in L.A., which ended up costing over $5 million in legal fees. We removed the founder from the company and tried to remake it. First we got out of the business of kiosks and sold off the marijuana vending licenses they had accumulated in Washington, Nevada, Oregon, and California. We bought a three-hundred-acre hemp farm in Pueblo, Colorado, installed CBD extraction equipment, and brought on farmers and a sales and leadership team to run it.

Once the board was cleared of wrongdoing, I resigned from the board and started thinking about how odd the human mind was. I was spending more time first thinking and then craving what I could have made, rather than feeling grateful for what I had. This seemed to be something others like me expressed as well. It's a version of the idea that "the grass is always greener on the other side of the fence." The bad news was that in my life I often tortured myself over what could have been: if I had gone to college, if I hadn't forgotten the signed Warhol lithograph, if I hadn't sold my Netflix stock so early, if I'd closed the Dish Network streaming deal, if I'd started at my own business.

I started reading studies about highly motivated/driven individuals and a couple of things struck me. Those who were workaholics and always trying to achieve more felt like they had to prove themselves worthy to one or both parents. For me it was my dad. I always wanted him to acknowledge my success, and just before he would have seen my success unmistakably, he passed away in 2001. I still, from time to time, leaf through the stock certificates of companies I had invested in and count up the millions of shares I owned. They were all worthless.

Shortly after I returned from my Southeast Asia trip, I received a call from Gregg Kaplan. He was on the board of Redbox's parent company now and had temporarily stepped into my former role as president of Redbox while they searched for a replacement. By now Redbox had completed the purchase of all of the assets of Blockbuster Express, including contracts with several large grocery chains like Safeway and Publix, contracts that represented a combined 2,600 locations and grocery sales of over $50 billion annually, plus over ten thousand automated DVD rental and sales kiosks. The acquisition price was $165 million, and the primary motive was to acquire the two remaining major grocery contracts. Within several months they removed all the Blockbuster kiosks and replaced them with Redbox kiosks. Even though the Blockbuster kiosks were more versatile, it was more efficient to run the business with one type of machine with the same software, spare parts, and training—in much the way that Southwest Airlines flies only one model, the Boeing 737.

Gregg asked me if I would manage the sales of these used Blockbuster kiosks to somebody else and get whatever I could, with the one proviso that they would not be sold in the United States or Canada. I was excited about the opportunity and quickly tracked down several of my regular contacts. At one point I needed to go inspect the inventory to assess the damage that removal might have caused and to see what spare parts were available. I will never forget entering one of two warehouses outside Cincinnati, Ohio. The ten thousand kiosks looked much like the scene at the end of the first Indiana Jones film, in which the lost ark is wheeled into a massive storeroom and the camera rises to reveal endless rows and piles of crates. That was my view looking over the top of thousands of kiosks. It was all a mess, with broken front panels and parts in piles.

I needed some former Blockbuster team members to sort it out and do an inventory. Fortunately, I had made friends with the folks at National Cash Register who had been managing Blockbuster Express. With a fair amount of wheeling and dealing I ended up selling six thousand kiosks to the team in Australia that owned the Blockbuster franchise there and the rest to two guys who operated a cheese and equipment logistics company in Mexico.

The Australian company had several thousand franchisees whose business was shrinking, and the company offered kiosks as a way to close marginal stores but still serve the customer base profitably. They did well. The Mexican group, Vidbox, made deals with Walmart and major grocers in Mexico and opened over four hundred locations, but alas it was too late. The move to Netflix streaming stymied all progress. However, with an ingenious pivot, they repurposed those kiosks and are now successfully vending CBD products in the United States.

Redbox essentially became one of the most successful kiosk design, manufacturing, and operating companies, which taught me much about the business of automated selling. Kiosks have some significant beneficial characteristics, including small footprints, low labor costs, and, when positioned properly, incredible profits and popularity with customers.

A San Francisco–based kiosk systems company called Cantaloupe Systems invited me to join the board and help their very capable cofounders and board members to craft the strategy to grow. Cantaloupe started by building software and hardware additions to old-fashioned vending machines that monitored and communicated inventory levels along with added credit card functionality. The company was well run but faced some major competition. We launched new beta projects that monitored document disposal containers and other products. Soon we grabbed the attention of one of their big challengers and received an attractive offer to sell the company. While I had been a part of acquiring other companies, this was my first experience with the sale of a company I was involved in to another.

As an investor, I had a lot to learn. In a real sense, despite having lived through the Silicon Valley dot-com bubble as well as making at least a dozen cash investments in publicly traded dot-coms, I was still like a babe in the woods when it came to evaluating a business idea. I would easily get passionate about whatever the founder was trying to solve for with their start-up and would want to help. After $25,000 here, $75,000 there, and $50,000 in some other place, I found myself in over my head. Before you knew it, I had invested in a golf-gambling tech company, a remote university printing kiosk, the curated gift box company Quarterly, and a book recommendation start-up called Booxby, even as I also became a limited partner (investor) in a "shared economy" fund and a crypto infrastructure fund.

About that time I received an invitation to connect on LinkedIn from a start-up founder named Khalid Itum. He was going to the Sundance Film Festival, as were my wife and I, so we agreed to meet. We met Khalid on a cold, snowy evening at a restaurant along the main street of Park City, Utah. He was helping manage a special dinner event, and Zamora and I joined them. These were great people, all smart and working at very cool companies, and clearly Khalid was highly respected by all. He told me about this company he was really excited about that he thought I might want to invest in. The company had developed technology that could scrape TV and movie content and add purchase links to scenes that contained clothing and jewelry, cars, and almost anything that could be bought. And this was just one of two or three possible revenue streams. I liked the people, was fascinated by the idea, and invested in the mid five figures. The company made a number of "pivots" to different business models but in the end shut down. As a minority investor, unless you make extra effort, you often don't know what the status of the company is until it's over.

This was not the last investment where I leapt before I really added up the pros and cons. I guess I had concluded that almost every idea could work if executed properly, and since I often overestimated the capabilities of people I met, I tended to believe in them. Even as recently as the year I'm writing this, 2021, I still find myself not taking a full methodical approach to my investments. One reason, of course, is that in all my past successes and failures, there was really no way to distinguish likelihood of success. At least that is my rough analysis.

Who would have known that a $50,000 investment into a cryptocurrency infrastructure fund would pay out well over $1.3 million over the last five years? Who would have known that befriending a random guy in Vegas would have led to Netflix, or a random call from some guys in Australia and Mexico would lead to $1.6 million in commissions on those Blockbuster kiosks? Over and over it has been those times where without any reason I have opened myself up to a new person and have had the ride of my life. Of course, more often than not, I wander down a deep and winding rabbit hole that ends up nowhere. But that's why I play the odds.

It was during this time I received a call from Marc Randolph, wondering what I thought about getting into public speaking. Marc explained that he was represented by an agency called BigSpeak out of Santa Barbara, California, and that he couldn't handle all the requests to give speeches at conferences and company meetings. After a great call with one of the principals, Ken Sterling, I was sold. Back in 1995 and 1997 I had given keynote speeches at my trade association's national conference. For one of them, which had a naval theme to play off Paramount's release of *The Hunt for Red October*, I came out onstage to an audience of three thousand video industry peers dressed in white naval officer uniforms. My introduction ended by showing a scene from *Ensign Pulver*, who was about to throw James Cagney's beloved potted palm off the side of their ship into the ocean; as I walked across the stage I saw a potted palm and threw it over the head of the camera operator off the stage.

I was so terrified about going up on stage. They say that most people have a greater fear of public speaking than they do of being naked in public. But as I wrote earlier, my son Joaquin had given me a hilarious *Far Side* cartoon that I still look at to get in the right mood before going on stage.

My engagement with BigSpeak has led to well over seventy speeches in Madrid, Porto, Dubai, Kuwait, Riyadh, Sydney, Melbourne, Buenos Aires, São Paulo, Mexico City, Punta Mita, Santiago, and just about every major city in the United States. I spoke at conferences for KPMG, Merck, Delta Dental, Oracle, Zendesk, SAP, Hershey, Capital One, RingCentral, and Bath & Body Works, as well as many tech conferences and universities.

And I learned so much and met so many fascinating people. Once I was on a weeklong speaking tour in Latin America with Wikipedia founder Jimmy Wales. We were speaking at the regional conferences for a multibillion-dollar transnational paper company and traveled on one of their corporate jets. Jimmy and I were together for quite a few hours and we had a chance to share some of our thinking on the world. Donald Trump had recently been elected and Brexit had just passed in the UK. Jimmy, though American, lives in the UK and shared with me how surprised he was that Brexit won. I felt the same shock that Trump had won as well.

After hours of discussing the why of it all, we came to one conclusion: that we all live within a bubble of like-minded people and read and watch and listen to news that reinforces our own existing concepts and beliefs. The result was that neither of us had exposure to people who thought differently about politics and the world than we did, so we had no sense of how many people thought that way. We parted ways after that week promising that each of us would force ourselves to watch the news services that came from the opposite angle. And in fact, Jimmy launched a news service to do just that.

While traveling all over the world I would generally add a day or two and find a nearby hiking trail. In 2017, I set a goal of hiking 1,500 miles and would hit the trail at 50 miles or so a week. By the first week of December, I had reached 1,450 miles. I had only 50 miles more to go and more than three weeks to complete them.

I remembered that I had learned that some cultures are said to always leave one thing undone or one small mistake in their artwork. I knew that if I did pass the 1,500-mile milestone, then the next time I would have to exceed 2,000 miles. Just as when I was about to drive into the only state I have not been to, South Carolina, but took the last exit from North Carolina to leave that undone, I also decided not to complete the 1,500-mile hiking goal. Maintaining big goals and the excitement of measuring your performance against them keeps me thrilled about waking up each day. In fact, if there is one thing I have learned, it is that if you do not feel that way then you are doing the wrong thing in life. Of course, 99.99 percent of people become content with that type of existence. I pray that you do not accept that.

My positioning as a speaker was as the "poor man's Marc Randolph." In other words, if you could not afford Marc, then I was your best choice to grab a little bit of that Netflix magic. And then Marc decided to focus on writing his book, so with his now much reduced availability, I had more speeches than even I could handle. But did I ever turn down even one of the twenty to thirty speeches I was doing every year? No.

I had started this period in my life by exploring the world and my own mind, continued by speaking all over the place, and gained a lot of experience by investing in companies. But one of those investments turned out to be more important and disruptive to my life than all of the others—and it would test the zen calm I had built up in India. That investment was in the ill-fated movie theater subscription venture MoviePass.

--- **TAKEAWAY** ---

In the same way that learning how to compartmentalize and prioritize your execution strategy is crucial for your business, the same is true about personal life. Compartmentalize so you can avoid the sense of being overwhelmed with so many things you need to do, and prioritize so that you make progress that builds on previous success. As simple as this sounds, your mind resists this kind of order and will find ways to convince you that you do not need to go this route. Deep understanding of your inner voices that, unbeknownst to you, are subconsciously battling with each other comes with long-term noble silence that allows these voices to surface. Once they surface, you can acknowledge them and resolve the disputes.

[9]

ZAZEN: MOVIEPASS VS. HOLLYWOOD

Samudya (The Truth of the Cause of Suffering)
We must personally explore why we are suffering: Why do we
hunger for success, or have greed for wealth, or whatever we
crave that we somehow believe we did not get?

MoviePass should have been an iconic disruptor along the
lines of Spotify or DoorDash. Instead, it will always be clas-
sified among the ranks of Tyco or Worldcom—as an epic failure.

Even the greatest ideas can't survive when speed outweighs
innovation. My time at MoviePass represents the only point in
my career where I failed to heed my Zen Buddhist teachings and
thought only about momentum and what could be rather than
how to get there.

I constantly think about what could have been and where I
went wrong.

Here's what happened.

In the spring of 2012, after my four-month trip to Southeast
Asia, and for the first time in many years, I really had nothing

going on. I felt rudderless with no job and no prospects. As I floated along a bit aimlessly, I started to feel afraid for my financial future.

My passion for start-ups and start-up leaders led me to invest and advise in a Polish social communications company that helped people connect with others with similar needs and interests in a very small perimeter and also helped businesses promote their services to potential customers within a square block or a square mile. I had also invested in a company that helped you find something great to read, a company that invested in crypto infrastructure companies, a fund that invested in "shared economy" start-ups, and a company that installed betting systems on golf courses. The passion of the cofounders behind these companies reminded me of the joy I felt myself at Netflix and at Redbox. I wanted to help with money, strategy, process, and hiring advice to help these amazing leaders experience the same exhilaration I had felt. The business model, the people, the go-to market strategy, and of course the funding.

Two of my kids were getting master's degrees, and there was still plenty of new pressure to provide for my family. Admittedly, I was in a pretty good place financially with enough to live on for the rest of my life. However, if I had to weather a huge catastrophe, I would suddenly find myself in a precarious situation.

I started looking around for fresh opportunities. Where was the next Netflix or Redbox? Who could best use my knowledge and experience?

During one of my Blue Bottle Coffee meetings with True Ventures's Tony Conrad, he told me about a seed investment and Round A funding of $1 million they had recently placed in a company called MoviePass. With the success of Netflix, Tony believed that a subscription service could work for movie tickets. He introduced me to the two founders, Stacy Spikes and Hamet Watt.

Stacy and Hamet's concept for MoviePass was to be a high-end service, very exclusive, that would take the hassle out of going to lots of movies at different theater chains for the moviegoing fanatic. It was priced between $40 and $50 per month. It was also targeted at film lovers who don't get to festivals like Sundance, Toronto, or Mill Valley where there are always incredible hidden gems. Certainly, many of these handcrafted original stories don't get attention like the big blockbusters distributed by major studios and backed by multimillion-dollar marketing campaigns, and I saw MoviePass as a way to increase viewership of those "film-festival-like" small but great movies.

When Tony asked me to advise MoviePass, one name entered my mind: Marc Randolph, who I always credited as being the founder of Netflix, and who was a genius when it came to marketing and product development. I believed that working together with Marc would offer MoviePass the fixes it so desperately needed.

Marc employed a detail-oriented process, tested his theories, and made proposals that required a specific execution. This contrasted with my style, which encourages product leaders to make their own decisions on product development. I then try to offer big-picture advice and put them in touch with strategic partners.

Together, we had both the macro and micro aspects of MoviePass's challenges covered and began to formulate a clear idea of what had to happen for the company to move forward. However, after three or four months, Marc called me and said, "I just can't handle this any longer! These guys just won't take any of my advice!

"They'll sit and listen," Marc continued. "But then the fact is they're not taking anybody's advice. They just keep doing the same old thing and that's why they're struggling to get above ten thousand in paid subscribers!"

Ten thousand paying MoviePass subscribers was still an impressive milestone, but the company had hit a wall. Tony as an investor was concerned that growth was stalled.

As for me, my big-picture advice was to lower the monthly price from $34.95 to around $14.95. I saw this as a mass-appeal service, and if it was priced low enough you could attract millions of movie fans. And similar to Netflix, it would take away the difficult decision in an à la carte entertainment service of deciding whether this film is worth $9.

Stacy and Hamet did not like that idea. They were just as stubborn with me as they had been with Marc.

Their perspective was that MoviePass was a kind of platinum card service for people who are willing to pay forty bucks a month. In New York, their price point was actually $49.95, which I also felt was way too expensive. With no common ground to be found on establishing a new, more accessible pricing model, Marc and I decided to give up on MoviePass.

But that turned out not to be the end of things.

Two years later, I was walking through the San Francisco airport when I got a call from Sam Englehart, one of the bigger investors in MoviePass. He had put in $1 million and had since grown incredibly frustrated with Stacy and Hamet. During this call, I learned that Stacy and Hamet were each paying themselves well even as the company was losing massive amounts of money each month.

Growth and financial progress had ceased under their leadership. But Sam's investment was actually a loan. He could call it in and Stacy and Hamet would then have thirty days to pay it back or, if they couldn't come up with the cash, Sam would take over the company as collateral for the loan.

Sam had heard that I had advised the company and that Stacy and Hamet had not taken my advice. He had learned of my recommendations for pricing and wholeheartedly supported this new direction. As he saw it, he could watch his investment just waste away or he could change course. Sam wanted to call in the loan and put me in charge as CEO.

I had always been in love with the concept of MoviePass and the idea of creating a model that would democratize movies for both customers and filmmakers. It would create bigger opportunities for films with smaller budgets, with less of a reliance on major studios and a bigger share of the box office for independent films. That idea continued to attract me.

Sam and I met in L.A. to plan the takeover, which started with calling in the loan. Stacy and Hamet now had a month to either pay him back or hand over the company to us.

Well, Stacy and Hamet were not giving up that easily. They actually raised another million before the deadline.

They'd connected with Chris Kelly, who was the former chief privacy officer and I believe the first general counsel at Facebook—one of the first twenty employees—and he was now living in the San Francisco Bay Area. He was part owner of the Sacramento Kings and had run—and lost—to Kamala Harris for attorney general of California. He was accomplished and smart, had a big interest in film, and was always looking for a new adventure.

When Stacy and Hamet approached him, MoviePass was a compelling prospect. Stacy and Hamet also offered Chris a chance to be a hero by describing how Sam was trying to steal the company out from under them.

I guess being a knight in shining armor appealed to Chris, because he forked over the million dollars and Hamet and Stacy were able to pay off Sam in the nick of time. Chris continued kicking in major amounts of cash, but he didn't ask how it was being used.

By 2015 I had put MoviePass out of my mind. But then I found myself at the Sundance Film Festival in Utah in January 2016 checking out some films, reminiscing, and drinking some great wine with Ted Sarandos, Marc Randolph, Patty McCord, Reed Hastings, and some other old buddies from Netflix.

Reed had bought an old converted Methodist church in Park City, and we were all hanging out there. While at Reed's place I received a call from my friend Khalid, who was at Chris Kelly's house not too far away. He suggested that Chris wanted to meet me and discuss MoviePass. It's a small world—especially in entertainment—and I now found myself on my way to meet with the guy whose cash had kept me out of the CEO seat at MoviePass.

From the second I walked in the door, it was as if Chris and I had known each other for years. We both shared a passion for movies and, more specifically, for independent films, which we viewed as an underserved part of the entertainment community. For hours, we talked about the right strategy for MoviePass.

"These guys running MoviePass just don't get it," Chris said despondently.

"It also doesn't help that you're essentially covering the company's burn rate equal to purchasing a Tesla each month," I answered. Chris shrugged, and we sat for a few moments in silence.

"Listen," Chris said. "Let's get you involved. Would you consider buying in?"

Chris offered me a chance to invest my own money and to essentially buy the title of CEO—an unusual offer. With a lot to think about, I left his house and spent the rest of the weekend trudging through the snow from theater to theater getting lost at the movies.

A few months later, Chris and I agreed to discuss making me the CEO of MoviePass.

Truthfully, I was honored that he viewed me as the person who could save MoviePass. Furthermore, this moment felt like the culmination of all my years in video stores working at the counter, talking to customers about movies and learning why they chose different movies and TV shows.

During my years at Netflix, I was helping to teach the team about the video rental industry, but in the end, Reed and Marc knew what they wanted to do. And at Redbox, we were renting two million movies a day, but most of the titles were big blockbusters. It was a lucrative business enterprise, but it didn't inspire me.

MoviePass was my moment to be the number one guy and to maybe also do some good for the movie business. Could we revitalize the independent film industry in the United States and around the world? Enough already with huge special effects and totally predictable stories and crappy remakes. This was a chance to get people back into theaters to see films they would otherwise never have heard of.

As we spoke, it was clear that Chris didn't want to fire the founders. He was just such a nice guy and didn't want to be the bastard. Instead he wanted me to take the helm and decide their fate. From my perspective, it was just business and I didn't mind being the bad guy, because cleaning house was often part of business.

We concluded our negotiation with an agreement for me to invest $250,000 of my own money, which was a smart requirement from Chris. If I had a significant amount of money invested, I was less likely to give up early and walk away from the company if things got tough.

Now officially on board, I sat down with Stacy and Hamet and the rest of the team—around ten people based in New York—with the goal of getting to know everybody and to try to understand each person's contribution to the company. I was ready to fire people if I needed to, but I was just as happy to keep everybody in place if we could outline a clear strategy for success. Stacy and I had a good working relationship at least until early 2018. He took the title of COO and ran the day-to-day business of operations, marketing, customer service, and HR. Hamet, who lived in Southern California, had always been a strategy guy, and since that was what I was doing, he left the company in October 2016.

The subscriber base was now hovering around twenty thousand individuals, and the monthly cost was still set at around forty bucks in New York City and $34.95 in cheaper markets.

I knew the prices were still much too high and represented a massive barrier of entry for new customers—and Stacy still disagreed.

I focused on researching different price points. I took everything I had learned at Netflix and at Redbox about the subscription model—and turning a profit—and spent most of my time analyzing, retesting, and changing the variables within the MoviePass model.

As I'd learned in my previous companies, in any subscription, there's always a magic price point where the cost of content becomes attractive to a large enough base. With enough sustained demand, the company creates revenue while finding ways to reinvest and expand services, all while remaining up-to-date with technology.

I studied a breakdown of consumers who go to movies and found that only about 11 percent of moviegoers went to more than eight movies a year. It was simple math: the quantity of consumers that a $34.95 monthly program appealed to was way too small.

With the help of Chris's friend Sanjay Puri, a former World Bank analyst, we tested price points and various offerings. There had to be a middle ground between a price that was too low to be profitable given how much content we were offering, and one that was too high and therefore wasn't compelling to enough subscribers. We tested $14.95 for up to two movies a month and then we tested $19.95 for a movie per day. We also tested different price points in different markets, like $24.95 in New York and $14.95 in the Midwest.

We even tried $89.95 per month, for which you could see all the movies you wanted in the most expensive market, including any 3D showing, IMAX film, and special screenings. After all the research, we were right back where we started: $14.95 offered consumers a really good deal and when adding other revenue streams could be profitable.

In the end, this was the proposition that we presented to Chris and the rest of the MoviePass team.

The $38 billion worldwide movie theater business begins at your local cinema. In the United States, that is just over $11 billion in revenue and 1.3 billion tickets sold annually, which has been relatively steady.

Twenty years earlier, in 1995, 1.2 billion tickets were sold. So the number of tickets sold is pretty close to flat. The growth has come from increases in ticket price. During the last twenty years, the average ticket price more than doubled to just under $9. And, as in many consumer businesses, a small percentage of consumers represent a significant share of tickets sold. In the movie theaters, around 36 million consumers buy over 50 percent of the tickets sold every year.

In the United States alone, studios spend up to $100 million marketing their biggest releases. In total, over four hundred films are released to US cinemas annually, which causes short runs and lack of awareness of most of these titles. While the creative communities in Hollywood—and around the country—make their films to be seen on the big screen, much of their content is viewed on smaller screens.

In this business, everyone faces challenges.

- The big challenge for frequent entertainment consumers? Going to the movies has become so costly that each choice is measured against the possible value of the experience. Consumers read reviews, listen to other consumers, and then see if they have the time to risk the film not living up to expectations and offering a return on investment.
- The big challenge for theater owners? Typically, after the opening weekend release of a film, many seats go empty.

That means that expenses for huge theaters rise as they simultaneously miss out on high-margin sales of snacks and drinks—concessions.

- The big challenge for the studios? With each release, they have to spend large amounts on inefficient mass media marketing since they are not able to collect direct contact and taste information from past customers of their movies.

MoviePass addressed each of these three constituencies.

For consumers, our unlimited plan and our plans for up to two or up to three movies per month allowed our subscribers to make movies a regular part of their entertainment choice. In addition, being a subscriber offered valuable benefits such as exclusive invitations to private movie screenings, guaranteed tickets to blockbuster openings, discounted access to movie soundtracks, digital copies, DVDs, movie posters, and much more.

For exhibitors, MoviePass subscribers went to the movies twice as often as before. This meant that our subscribers also drove sales of high-margin concessions. MoviePass subscribers also helped fill those many empty seats after the first weekend of a title release.

For studios, MoviePass provided data and marketing services that improved the ability of a studio to identify likely customers. Additionally, since most of our subscribers went twice as often after becoming a subscriber, and half of our movie transactions were incremental to the industry, MoviePass was increasing nationwide movie ticket sales by over 5 percent. On an $11 billion annual business, that 5 percent added over $500 million to the till, with half of that going to the studios. Plus since our subscribers doubled their purchases of high-margin concessions, the theaters were raking in close to $1 billion. By the way, that is exactly the percentage of the national box office that was purchased by MoviePass in the first six months of 2018—which was, by the way, the first year in many that box office ticket sales increased.

That was our pitch. And even as we spent our days endlessly testing price points and offerings, we were pitching investors nearly every night. Sanjay had a vast network across the United States, while my name and reputation—as well as Chris Kelly's— carried a lot of cachet in this space. Sanjay and I were meeting with at least two or three potential investors every week—anybody with a pulse and a wallet—for almost a year: SoftBank executives, high-net-worth angels, and venture capitalists from Los Angeles, San Francisco, Silicon Valley, Chicago, and New York.

There was no shortage of interested investors. But over the course of a hundred pitch meetings, nobody seemed to under-stand the value from a consumer's perspective. They questioned how many people we could get if we lowered the price. And, if we lowered the price, potential investors couldn't understand why people wouldn't overuse the product. There also was a lot of concern regarding the potential for losses on movie tickets and our ability to offset them with alternative revenue streams. If we lowered the price to $14.95—which was what we wanted to do—these investors were worried that we'd be losing $10 to $15 per subscriber monthly if our average subscriber went to two or more movies each month. How were we going to make up that lost money?

Meanwhile, I was working with Stacy to reduce wasteful spending so the company could stay afloat. He was also being a good soldier and making the best of an awkward situation. Stacy had always told me that the big challenge in the company was having enough money to fund a growing subscriber base. In fact, that was his main pushback when it came to lowering the price. He knew about all of the subscription services out there—especially the all-you-can-eat subscription services. I explained to Stacy that the first people you attract are the overeaters who believe that they can really save money in this service. However, you find that over time those overeaters are lessening their consumption each month, and you start attracting the casual moviegoer who is looking for convenience.

If we applied the same logic to the 11 percent of moviegoers I mentioned earlier, they might start at six movies a month. Then, a couple months later, they're down to four and then down to three. We thought we could get the heavy users down to around two movies a month. Then the other 89 percent of consumers—who only go to four movies a year—well, we thought we could get them up to one movie or three-quarters of a movie each month and they would be thrilled to still be getting a deal, being able to see unlimited movies and not having to face the dreaded decision of whether a movie is worth it. They would indeed start to consume more but, more importantly, we would be able to find lots of additional revenue streams where we could generate money from them—provided we had a big subscriber base.

We knew that we eventually could earn advertising money from the studios to pitch movies to our subscriber base—especially those smaller studios where we were driving huge increases in consumption. We also knew we could get money from ancillary sales, where we could enable the subscriber to use our credit card to buy coffee before the movie or pay the babysitter. For those types of services, you're typically earning around an incremental 7 percent from the average consumer.

Typically, moviegoers were spending around $50 before or right after setting foot in the theater. We believed we could eventually get a piece of the concession sales from some exhibitors, and we believed that as the customer base grew, we could get bigger and bigger discounts on our cost for providing movie tickets. After all, AMC and Cinemark sold packets of tickets at Costco for 25 percent off, while we would be buying millions of dollars' worth of tickets. (Eventually, MoviePass bought roughly $300 million worth of tickets in one year.)

Not only could we lower our costs on tickets by 25 percent, we also were confident that we could earn a dollar per ticket in advertising money, which is what we believed Fandango earns per ticket—and we thought we could get three or four dollars a month for being a part of a frequent coffee-or-dinner-afterward program.

We were also convinced that we could get other types of revenue built around data and the ability to help studios understand customer demand. This valuable information might also help them drive consumption without overspending on marketing. We knew that data was extremely valuable and that we could learn not only about our customers but also about customers who go to different movie theaters: AMC versus Cinemark versus other smaller brands. After all, neither movie exhibitors nor studios have a direct relationship with all of the cinema consumption of the typical moviegoing customer, but we would.

At the time, we had received a number of small investments that kept us pretty much at break-even from a cash flow perspective, as we had gotten the burn rate down to under $50,000 a month. Still, we couldn't muster enough money to launch a marketing campaign or create a little breathing room.

It felt like every turn led us into a brick wall, and by the start of summer in 2017, the money that was coming in was only extending the company's ability to keep going but not making a real difference. I didn't want to take any more investments, and I was ready to call it quits.

Then I got a MoviePass-saving phone call: our pitch managed to get the attention of David Kaplan, managing partner at Madison Global Partners. "I've got a couple of investors I want to introduce you to who might see a strategic advantage to investing in MoviePass," he explained. And that turned into a meeting with a very different kind of investor.

David Kaplan set up a time for Sanjay and me to meet with Ted Farnsworth, an investor based in New York. Ted ran a company called Helios and Matheson, where the primary business revolved around an app that helped insurers identify areas that had a high amount of crime. If somebody was buying a new house, they could use the app to access a heat map based on the types of crime within a certain radius. However, like me, Ted also had a passion for film.

Based on our previous challenges with getting big investors on board, we went into this meeting with Ted with limited expectations. Little did we know that Ted would represent a breath of fresh air.

As we explained the concept of MoviePass, Ted's eyes lit up and he started sharing all these ideas with us: new marketing approaches and how we could incorporate all these other revenue streams from advertising and data sales. He, like us, also wanted to set up a process to use the MoviePass credit card to buy food before or after the movie.

Ted's background really fascinated me. One of the companies he founded was called the LaToya Jackson Psychic Network. This was before the internet, so you called this number, paid $5 charged to your phone bill or a credit card, and got a psychic reading. Ted explained that they generated more than $100 million a year from just that business.

Bottom line: This guy knew how to translate tech and media ideas into profitable enterprises. He was the right guy for Movie-Pass; he had this really amazing sense for how to market a product to a consumer. And, instead of spending lots of money marketing, he wanted to come up with an idea that was so good that, by word of mouth, we'd attract tens of thousands of subscribers without spending huge amounts on advertising.

A couple days later, I received a proposal from Ted. He believed that MoviePass could be a great business, and he offered $25 million to buy 51 percent of MoviePass with an option to buy more at a valuation to be mutually determined.

Additionally, there was a $2 million bonus for MoviePass shareholders (including me) if we got to 150,000 subscribers within eighteen months of signing the deal.

We met in his office on the seventy-fifth floor of the Empire State Building facing north, looking out over Central Park, and that's where we hammered out the fine points in an all-night negotiation.

With enough cash and with the right backer, in August 2017, we launched the product nationwide at $9.95 a month. Why $9.95? Well, it was a dollar above the average cost of a ticket in the United States, so we believed that customers would think, "Even if I just go to one movie a month it's worth it," and it was the price many services such as Netflix were charging. The best aspect of this price point was that it meant we could save millions of dollars typically spent marketing a service like this due to incredible PR. The plan was to raise the price by the end of 2019, when we forecast five million subscribers and we would be offsetting any losses on the service with ad sales, data sales, and other revenue. As you'll soon see, that generated a new set of problems. We went from the challenges of lack of growth to the challenges of hypergrowth.

For $9.95, a customer could see all the movies they wanted, up to one per day, at about 90 percent of the movie theaters across the United States. We also didn't need an agreement with the movie theaters to sell their tickets, since we were paying the full price on the MoviePass MasterCard—the whole process was really invisible to the theater. Or so we thought.

Of course, we hoped that eventually we would get the same 25 percent discount on those tickets that theater chains like AMC and Cinemark offered to individual customers who bought packets of tickets at Costco. Still, in the beginning, we were prepared to overspend to prove to the theaters that we could be valuable.

Indeed, the $9.95 was a deal that most people described as too good to be true. On the day in August that the new pricing model was announced, our systems—like many start-ups with a surge in popularity—crashed. In fact, we were offline for about four hours overnight following the $9.95 announcement. Despite that, when we came in the following morning, we saw— Holy Toledo!—that over fifty thousand paying customers had signed up in the first twenty-four hours. Meanwhile, Ted and I were on various news shows promoting the product on the second day of availability and, as we were talking to CNN, CNBC, and Bloomberg, another fifty thousand subscribers joined the service.

To understand what happened next, you need to know a little about how we actually ran the MoviePass program.

Once a consumer signed up, we created a customized Master-Card debit card with the user's name and the MoviePass logo on it. It had no money or credit until we at MoviePass turned it on for a specific amount of money to be used at a specific type of merchant, namely a movie theater. Our banking partner, Vantiv, created these cards and limited their use to companies that had "movie theater" as their category code.

The customer would use our app to choose a movie theater and a movie to go to. And when the customer got close to the theater, because of our geo-fencing tech around the theater, the credit would automatically flow to the card to pay for tickets, and there would be just enough money to buy those tickets at the price that the theater charged. If the customer did not purchase the tickets within a thirty-minute window, the credit was removed from the card. MoviePass handled the bill.

Recall that we had just gotten a surge of fifty thousand subscribers based on the news coverage. The issue with this early success was that we only had about seventy-five thousand card blanks ready to print the name of each customer on. I immediately got on the phone with Vantiv and with MasterCard to see just how quickly we could get more cards made. We weren't talking about manufacturing a simple plastic rectangle. Our cards had all this embedded technology alongside the protection of a regular credit card. Unfortunately, there are only three or four places where these types of cards could be made in the United States, and the capacity was basically thirty thousand per week. I knew we were going to blow through that limitation in a matter of days.

Facing major delays and a backlog of orders, we had to immediately get a second facility authorized by MasterCard and up and running in a day or two. To get started, we paid them $50,000 to transport half a million blank cards to a new facility located in L.A.

On the third day of offering the $9.95 deal, we got another fifty thousand subscribers. I was shocked and surprised that we hit the 150,000 subscriber milestone so quickly.

Keep in mind that hitting 150,000 subscribers in under eighteen months also triggered the shareholders' $2 million bonus. Not one of us expected to achieve that milestone in three days. And the demand didn't stop. Every day, we were getting ten thousand to twenty thousand new subscribers and shipping out as many cards as fast as we could. Of course, despite the fact that our new subscribers' first-month clock did not start until they both received the membership card and activated it, we were receiving hundreds of complaints daily from customers. By December we had caught up with the backlog, and from then on we were fulfilling new subscriber sign-ups within a week.

Over the next couple months, we surpassed one million subscribers. MoviePass became the fastest-growing subscription service in the history of entertainment. For reference, Netflix took thirty-nine months to hit one million subscribers. Even Spotify took longer—more than four months—to get to one million subscribers.

Everything was great until the counsel at AMC threw a wrench into the works.

Adam Aron was president and CEO at AMC Theatres, the largest chain of theaters in the world. He had been running AMC for a couple of years and had previously held executive roles working across travel and hospitality for Vail Resorts, Norwegian Cruise Line, United Airlines, and Hyatt Hotels.

AMC's counsel sent us a cease-and-desist regarding the operation of MoviePass in AMC theaters.

The note surprised me. When I started at MoviePass in 2016, we had already had a deal with AMC to jointly determine what the impact of MoviePass was on their customers. In two markets—Denver and Boston—we established a partnership where we both would provide a mutually agreed-upon third-party analytics company with all the customer information from our MoviePass subscribers, so AMC could analyze data for people who were also in AMC's movie loyalty club. The study identified thousands of MoviePass customers who had also been AMC loyalty members and revealed that they went to twice as many movies after becoming a MoviePass subscriber. With that, their consumption of purchased concessions more than doubled as well.

There was a huge benefit to AMC thanks to MoviePass subscribers. If an individual suddenly starts seeing twice as many movies in a given month, that was also positive for concession sales, and popcorn and soda that have 80 percent profit margins. AMC and MoviePass were aligned in that more tickets equaled more hungry and thirsty consumers buying goods at a more profitable margin. As we both saw the real benefit, we had continued to explore an expansion of the relationship under the previous president of AMC, Gary Lopez.

However, now that Adam was running the show, I concluded that they saw the $9.95 price point as a way for us to take the direct relationship they had with their customer and thus create value for MoviePass and not AMC. AMC forced us to shut down our study in the Boston and Denver markets and disabled our access to the AMC movie schedule API for use on the MoviePass app.

Our lawyers informed us that while they could prevent us from using their software data interface and that they could also stop us from contributing data to this third-party aggregator, they couldn't stop MoviePass customers from continuing to buy tickets. It would be challenging for them to discriminate based on which version of MasterCard was allowed.

Look, we were paying for every ticket. It's not like we were getting any discount.

At the time, we were in the midst of this incredible growth. We were struggling to supply cards fast enough to the tens of thousands of customers who were signing up every day. Now I had to find a whole new source for showtime data for the largest chain of theaters in the nation, since AMC had cut off our access to their API. I also had to extricate myself from this third-party analysis that I had thought would serve as a linchpin for our business as well as for the business of AMC. And, as our demand was soaring, we were trying to service customers who all want to see movies within the same period of time. Plus, with every delay, we were getting slammed with huge amounts of complaints.

And right around then, my wife and I decided to separate after forty years together.

Every day was filled with solving one problem or another and checking that off and moving on to the next crisis.

Still, in the midst of all this negativity, there was hope. We started receiving calls from directors, producers, and small distribution companies that were excited and all saw MoviePass as a great marketing vehicle to drive more awareness for their films.

Were we heading in the right direction?

Amid the growth, the number of movies viewed by each subscriber was dropping just as we needed it to in order to make the economics work. The average new customer was coming in and watching around 3.8 movies in their first month. That number dropped to 3.4 in the second month and was then down to 2.8 in the third. While the whole goal was to get people to the movies, we needed them to do so in a way that was sustainable within our model. Ultimately, we still had to subsidize a wave of demand, and we were drawing closer to the biggest couple months of movie releases with Thanksgiving and Christmas. We knew that the holiday movie slate would drive up consumption and, while we were collecting $10 a month, we'd likely continue having to spend $30.

That left us with $20 to cover per customer each month. With a million subscribers, and the holidays around the corner, we could be looking at $20 million just in monthly customer costs.

We stayed afloat by continuing to raise more money and by selling more of the company to Ted Farnsworth's company, Helios and Matheson. This established an increasing valuation for MoviePass as a company. While we had sold 51 percent of the company at $25 million—which implied a total valuation in the neighborhood of $49 million—we negotiated a higher value for the remaining 49 percent.

We got $5 million from Helios and Matheson at a valuation that implied that MoviePass was worth around $100 million. Subsequent investments led to them owning 92 percent of the company before the end of the year with a valuation of over $200 million.

Of course, there wasn't going to be an endless lifeline from Ted, so we looked to offset costs by selling annual memberships. With an advance in payment, we'd have more money up front and would also offer the customer a big discount. We believed that this would give us enough time to get further ticket discounts, greater advertising revenue, and more to get to the break-even point.

We settled on a Black Friday campaign with a soft launch a few days before Thanksgiving, and the response was phenomenal. We sold approximately one hundred thousand annual subscriptions at a $100 fee, which was a 20 percent discount off the monthly rate.

With this influx of cash, the MoviePass team was feeling really thankful. However, that feeling was fleeting. The cash we were counting on was not actually going to go into our bank account.

Right after the Thanksgiving holiday, our credit card processor explained that they wanted to hold on to all the cash from these new yearly subs. They were skeptical that our story would end well and they anticipated that, if and when the company folded, they'd be on the hook for $10 million based on a 100 percent refund of the yearly subs.

"Ultimately, we're taking all the responsibility and all of the risk with not much upside," they explained.

We negotiated back and forth for a couple of days, and eventually they agreed to give us 10 percent up front. This meant that each time we sold an annual subscription for $100, we would get $10 with the other $90 in an escrow of sorts.

As it turned out, this was the beginning of a set of events that resulted in the fall of MoviePass.

However, a crucial boon came from a deal with Costco that Chris Kelly had facilitated. Luckily for us, Costco wanted to offer a bundled subscription service that included both MoviePass and Fandor, Chris's streaming service for indie films. We offered a yearly membership to Costco customers for $90 and they allowed us to keep $70, which we were thrilled with. Unlike our credit card company, Costco was giving us a majority of the revenue from the sales.

The Costco program began in early December, and by Christmas they had sold around 280,000 annual memberships. That's the money that got us through the winter.

Despite the static from the credit card company, some bad reviews, a few unhappy subscribers, and AMC throwing sand in our gears, we were still alive and decided to go out drinking to celebrate.

As it happened, we were stumbling around Times Square on a super cold night and thought it would be fun to swing by the AMC movie theater on 42nd Street. We huddled underneath the big marquee, bathed in the lights of the theater, and snapped a picture with all of us holding up our MoviePass cards in one hand and flipping off AMC with the other.

If this thing was going to work, I guess we needed a little bit of a "fuck you" mentality. It was us against the big guys.

It was a harrowing time. I felt like a samurai warrior with a whole slew of assailants coming at me. But living through a continuing crisis was something I thought I could deal with.

In fact, I had no idea just how bad it was going to get.

TAKEAWAY

Decisions made in desperation to save your baby, while gratifying in the short term, tend not to be based on a thoughtful evaluation of the pros and cons. Sometimes it's better to give up and close the business. But not being a quitter makes that so, so difficult. How is it possible to know for sure when to call it quits on your start-up? It's a lesson no one wants to learn, but many of us must.

[10]

GREAT HUMILITY/MOVIEPASS: FROM AUDACITY TO HUMILIATION

Magga (The Truth of the Path
That Frees Us from Suffering)
There is resolution of our suffering as we acknowledge that we
and only we decide whether we suffer or not. In the end it is all
a craving for something we do not have, and truly in the end it
does not matter. This does not end until you replace suffering
with that which does matter.

Every day seemed to throw new challenges at us at MoviePass. I
was determined to find a way to turn our incredible growth
into success. But the problems kept getting bigger.

By mid-December 2017, MoviePass had added over one million paid subscribers. We were adding ten thousand or more each
day and had ramped up our new membership card and package
mailings to 80 percent of new sign-ups within days. Every team in
the company was scrambling every hour of the day.

IT was daily adding server capacity to process hundreds of thousands of transactions where just five months prior, the new daily numbers were in the hundreds.

The product team almost daily identified new and clever ways our subscribers were figuring out how to abuse our terms and conditions. They were lending the account membership card to friends; making the card work remotely; reserving tickets in time windows that opened a window to purchase two tickets daily instead of one; buying tickets every day for five days and then turning them in for credit at the theater and then bringing four friends to see an opening night blockbuster. The fraud was endless.

The HR team was hiring weekly for marketing, operations, and accounting. Every department needed more.

The hardest part was money. While we had originally sold 51 percent of the company for $25 million to Helios and Matheson, we received only $15 million of that; the last two payments were contingent on an initial public offering (IPO). The $2 million shareholder bonus for passing 150,000 subscribers meant less now that Helios and Matheson owned almost all the shares. Ted's company had invested around $165 million in MoviePass, and every dime went toward subsidizing early users and the uncovered $20 of consumption per subscriber.

Nothing seemed to work other than raising more money. At this point all the new money was loans from Helios and Matheson, which were rising from $5 million weekly to $10 million by June 2018. We were truly riding the rocket ship into space while repairing and building the navigation system, tinkering with the propulsion system, and learning to fly—all at the same time. We were increasing capacity, trying to reduce fraud, and turning PR news coverage into sign-ups. But besides all these negatives many positives were taking place. We were signing up theaters that were giving us discounts, we were generating hundreds of thousands of dollars monthly in ad sales and through brand partners, and we were soon to roll out our partnership with food sellers.

Meanwhile, Sanjay was in charge of keeping bills paid and making sure that we received enough money each day and each week while paying off all the different constituents like Vantiv; keeping our banker happy; and at the same time looking for alternatives like a buyer or a bigger investor into MoviePass.

We had the classic problem that many successful high-growth start-up companies have faced and survived—the cash crunch. For example, Spotify burned through well over $1 billion before it started turning into positive cash flow. Our model was not unlike many other "all-you-can-eat" subscription services. We needed to go beyond the early adopters who had voracious appetites to a more average moviegoing public that would bring our average costs down. We were digging out from a hole in which the December 2017 subscribers were averaging 2.5 movies a month at $11 per ticket: many of our customers came from the coasts, where ticket prices were higher than the average, and so we were losing about $17 per month per subscriber. We knew that if we could get the average down to 1.2 movies a month at an average cost of $8.50 per ticket (the industry average of $8.50), we could break even on the subscription and then monetize all the other values we had.

The ancillary revenues and cost reductions would include advertising, partnerships, bigger discounts on tickets, and figuring out how to repurpose our membership card and our account for purchasing things like babysitting before going to the movies and getting a cup of coffee before the movie at your local Starbucks— all ways to earn a few dollars a month per subscriber.

Bernadette McCabe, who ran our cinema partnerships, was hard at work with her team signing up new theaters, mostly small independents who would accept our account with a discount. They were looking for ways to compete against the big three, AMC, Cinemark, and Regal, which represented a good 60 percent of all ticket sales. The indies offered ambiance, food, and drink, along with sound and picture quality equal to that of the big chains, but still needed an edge. Many saw MoviePass as that edge.

Typically, we were getting a 25 percent discount off the cost of the tickets from these indie theaters, but even better, we were able to work with them electronically so that the customers could pick the showtimes, and even pick their seats, within the MoviePass app. The customer would receive a QR code and didn't need to use the MasterCard MoviePass card that operated like a turn-on and turn-off debit card. For the theater owner, we doubled frequency of visits and doubled our subscribers' spending on profitable concessions.

Bernadette and her team were making great progress over that month of January as she was signing up retail cinema houses such as Brian Schultz's Studio Movie Grill, which had twenty or so theaters in the Southwest and was poised for much bigger growth. Brian became a big believer in our mission and also an investor.

Brian was one of the few in the theater business who realized innovation was lacking in the industry. Other than food and a better viewing environment, the pricing model for theaters hadn't changed in a long time.

At the same time Khalid Itum, who ran our studio relationships, was building advertising revenue streams, particularly for small films such as *I, Tonya*. At that time, we were typically buying around 3 to 5 percent of the tickets nationwide of most movies, but for films we promoted that made less than $20 million at the box office, we were averaging about 25 percent of the tickets. We estimated that we were adding several million dollars to the box office of these films.

Khalid's business development team was having great success getting various studios to pay for this added exposure on our site. This wasn't rocket science. When you have a customer who has no incremental cost for following your suggestions, they do so at many times more than would be typical for even the best targeted direct advertising. We found that roughly 17 to 18 percent of the customers to whom we recommended a small unknown film actually purchased the ticket and went to the film. And more often than not, they loved the film and told their friends to go see it, generating a full-price customer for the studio.

This was a huge benefit to the movie theater business that was trying everything possible not to rely so much on the big tentpole blockbusters. Remember, theaters would pay anywhere from 80 to 90 percent of the revenue in the first couple weeks of release on the big blockbusters to the studios, whereas for small independent films it could be as little as 50 percent. Our subscribers tended to go to the movies on weekdays and even during the day, when 80 percent of seats would otherwise be empty, which was a dream for most theater operators.

During this time, we started seeing a terrible pattern where our average cost of tickets at certain theaters was way above what it should have been. I believed that some theater chains might not be giving the senior discounts or the generally available Tuesday or weekday and daytime discounts that our customers deserved. We saw indications that some chains might be charging MoviePass cardholders a higher price than we thought they should. Eventually we hired a third-party field team to test this, and they provided some evidence that convinced us to consider doing more research. But in the end we decided not to do this, as it could have been random mistakes by ticket sellers at the box office. This was a harbinger of trouble to come.

We were adding new strategic partners all the time. Sanjay and I had reached out to Joe Robinson at iHeartRadio knowing that they could be a good partner in selling subscriptions, probably giving us much more than 90 percent of collected revenue. iHeartRadio saw the potential of bundling their Spotify-like service with MoviePass as a way to create a competitive product. They viewed their huge radio advertising operation as a way to generate ad revenue and bounty revenue from selling the bundled MoviePass/iHeart music service.

In the midst of all this, Khalid had started to prepare for a big MoviePass event at the upcoming Sundance Film Festival. Before I knew it, operating on his own, he had rented a twenty-three-thousand-square-foot house right on the edge of Sundance and had hired a high-end caterer to support the several big parties he had planned for the house. For the next two weeks we partied with celebrities and directors and other moviemakers, along with a big team from both MoviePass and our parent company Helios and Matheson.

Khalid had created a great program for the MoviePass Sundance house. One of the things we did was a retrospective on the early days of Netflix with Marc Randolph and me. It was such a fun and enjoyable time with Marc reminiscing. It reminded me of how many things I learned from him and how often I wished I could reach out to him for advice. I realized that the reason I don't is that I'm sure he's going to tell me something that I disagree with, and what's worse is I know he will be right.

Both Ted and Khalid believed that these big marquee events that garnered huge social media and PR exposure were good for business. I was much more frugally minded and wanted us to focus on spending in those areas that would generate new subscribers who were lower-volume users, along with technology aimed at reducing fraud and building ancillary revenue streams—instead of parties. Unfortunately, Khalid and Ted went off on their own without me to plan the next big party at Coachella, where they managed to spend well over $1 million on an event that in my perspective really had no connection with our business. I was so upset that I didn't attend and just wanted to stay clear of it. This was becoming the start of a somewhat dysfunctional relationship between me and a number of the folks in the company. Even if they reported to me, if they didn't like my guidance they went behind my back to Ted to get what they wanted.

I can tell you that if you have two leaders or two cofounders, one of them absolutely must be the final decision maker and not for a second defer to a coleader, as the organization will ultimately find a way to manipulate the process. I found myself beginning to emotionally disconnect with the business, and I started losing faith in our future.

Around this time Rich Gelfond, the president of IMAX, reached out to us and wanted to meet. Rich's office was around fifteen minutes away, very close to our 35th and Madison office. We arrived right after lunch. Rich is a portly, relatively short man with a tough but direct demeanor. The first thing that Rich said was, "I have heard you are either the worst thing that has happened to our industry or the best." He then went on to say that when IMAX launched, they too were considered with skepticism, and he wanted to hear "straight from the horse's mouth" where we were coming from. I liked his demeanor, I liked his attitude, and I liked just how blunt and up front he was.

After an hour or so of conversation, I believed he had concluded that we were good for the industry and were not understood by his colleagues in the business. It was clear to me that he had had numerous conversations with theater owners, studios, and the trade association leaders about MoviePass. After the meeting he instructed the head of marketing for IMAX to develop a partnership that had two elements: to launch an IMAX-branded subscription plan and to work out a potential investment.

Khalid was of course in charge of detailing this partnership, but as I was starting to learn, as hard as Khalid worked to finalize these deals, our company had too many naysayers in the industry to move forward. I found that whether it was his involvement in the iHeart deal or with the other advertisers and small studios, despite Khalid's exhaustive understanding of all the details involved in a negotiation, many deals would eventually fall apart. And that's what happened with IMAX.

Eventually I found out that Rich would become a detractor of MoviePass after reading this quote in the media from him: "Someone told me they consider MoviePass to be a bad car accident that needs to be towed off the road. And I agree with that."

By April when the CinemaCon convention in Las Vegas gathered all the theater owners from around the world together, we sensed that something or someone had galvanized a coalition of major players against MoviePass. Even though we ended up signing over two thousand screens from independent theater houses, we found all the big guys not wanting to make deals with us.

One night during the CinemaCon event, I was invited to a VIP cocktail reception before an evening benefit. I walked in with Ted Farnsworth and our general counsel, Kevin Friedman. We were dapper in our tuxedos and as we entered the room, we saw Tom Cruise on the other side of the room. Not far from Cruise I saw the CEO of AMC, Adam Aron, who, as you'll recall from the previous chapter, had severed our multiyear test relationship in Denver and Boston. Between Adam and me was a thick crowd of theater industry stalwarts and since we had never met face-to-face, I thought this would be a good opportunity to introduce myself.

I of course had heard he was not a very nice person but I hoped a personal touch could possibly mend bridges and reform what had once been a good relationship with AMC. After all, we were now spending $15 million to $20 million a month at AMC theaters. The thick crowd of people milling around were all trying to maneuver themselves in front of Tom Cruise to say hello and describe how much they admired him. I took one look at Ted and said, "Hey look, there's our friend Adam Aron." Ted knew immediately what I was going to do and said, "Oh my God, don't do it!"

Kevin started smiling knowingly as I headed toward Adam. Behind my back I could almost feel Ted and Kevin holding their breath as I approached him. Adam is relatively tall, stout, and balding. He was talking with a couple of other people who looked like executives and also maneuvering to get near Tom Cruise, who I'm sure he knew quite well.

I came up to him and I said, "Hi, Adam, I'm Mitch." "Oh," he responded, "you are the one that keeps lying to the press." I asked him to explain, and he said that I had told the press that he had called an emergency board meeting at AMC in August to respond to MoviePass's new price point. I could tell I was not going to make progress, so I explained that I had not said that to the press and asked him if instead, could we talk about the positives? "No," he said bluntly, and turned away.

I looked back at Ted and Kevin, who were having a great laugh, and walked back over to their friendly slaps on the back for my bravery in facing up to the enemy. But Adam's reaction was a huge slap in the face to me, and it reminded me how often I've seen the incumbent players in businesses be blind to opportunity that comes from innovation. They are super protective of what they have, as opposed to looking at what the customer might want. I wasn't surprised but I was disappointed by the arrogance of his response. Of course Adam is still running AMC and our company filed for bankruptcy, so I guess he won.

We had so much going on in 2018 on many fronts. Earlier in the year, our parent company had purchased Moviefone from AOL. AOL had acquired Moviefone from its founders for $388 million in 1999 but had failed to turn it into the consumer movie info "go-to" site it had envisaged. You might remember that, prior to the internet, Moviefone was the dial-up service 777-FILM, lampooned on *Seinfeld* when Kramer started receiving wrong-number calls from people wanting to know movie schedules. Russ Leatherman, one of the cofounders and the voice of 777-FILM, was excited to work with us and build Moviefone back into a player.

Even as much as it had fallen from grace, Moviefone was still generating $4 million to $5 million in annual ad revenue, and we believed we could make it even bigger. We had this great opportunity to talk to moviegoers about entertainment and showtimes and drive people to MoviePass for their tickets, turning Moviefone into a feeder site for us.

As if things weren't already too complicated around this time, we had interest from Ari Emanuel at William Morris Endeavor to take a majority ownership interest in MoviePass. Ari and I started meeting on a fairly regular basis and strategized a dozen times or more on the phone about an integration into his multibillion-dollar agency group. He even had me speak to his entire organization about the potential of incorporating MoviePass into the William Morris Endeavor organization.

This was one of those times where I was ready to sell at a very modest price and fight for the future with a strong partner like Ari. Ari's companies represented over half of all the stars, directors, and writers in Hollywood, and in addition he had a huge worldwide entertainment event business including wine and food festivals. He shared with me his idea to make MoviePass the beginning of a subscription package to all his different events.

Unfortunately, Ted saw huge dollar signs and negotiated too hard, asking for too much money. Ari wanted to give us what he called "schmuck money," which essentially was to accept a low up-front price and get paid a lot more if we do well together. I was ready to take this offer, but Ted wanted several hundred million up front in cash, which Ari was unwilling to do. Eventually, after several months of negotiating, the deal fell through.

Landmark Theatres, a theater group co-owned by Mark Cuban and Todd Wagner with fifty-three high-end movie theaters around the United States, had become one of our strongest partners. We were integrated into their point-of-sale systems and were receiving significant discounts on cost of tickets. Even better for them, we were adding around $2 million weekly to their gross sales. Todd reached out to Ted and me and suggested that we discuss buying Landmark, since he and Mark had reached the end of their interest in the space. We joined in on the banker-led process in what was a modest bidding war to acquire the company. Meanwhile our subscribers were enhancing the value of Landmark, which boosted interest from competitors. In the end we won the bid in late July. As it turned out, before we could close the deal, it fell apart because of lack of financing.

As if this wasn't enough on our plate, we decided to begin to co-produce movies. We knew that for small films, especially those making less than $20 million at the box office, we could drive increased consumption, and add as much as $4 million to $8 million to the box office gross. Oftentimes that would mean the difference between success and failure of a film. Of course, filmmakers saw this partnership with MoviePass as a great opportunity to get their project greenlit and ensure at least modest box office results. The first movie we got involved with was called *American Animals*. It's a great film about four University of Kentucky college students and is based on a true story. These four losers decided that they were going to steal the most valuable book in the world, which was in the university library. It was an original folio of Audubon's drawings of birds.

We decided to have a huge red-carpet event with the actors and directors and other producers in New York City. We were partnering with Oasis Pictures, founded by Randall Emmett and George Furla. Often people have told me that Randall Emmett is the real-life person who the character Turtle from *Entourage* is patterned after. According to the story, he and Mark Wahlberg were friends in Philly and came out together to Hollywood to make it big.

For sure, Randall is one of the most entertaining guys you would ever want to spend a couple of hours with. He was constantly yelling and screaming and laughing at the top of his lungs. You know, the kind of classic Hollywood bad boy who is a character as well as being incredibly creative, smart, and one of the best negotiators I have ever known. I was once on a private plane flying with him and a few Helios and Matheson staff members from L.A. to Miami, when I heard Randall up in the cockpit trying to get the pilot to navigate out of turbulence, in between calls to ground control negotiating a better refueling price. He succeeded on both causes.

The red-carpet event we held in New York for *American Animals* was a huge success. The theater was full of new fans of

MoviePass, and the press wrote about how MoviePass would rein-vigorate the indie film industry. Things were getting heady as we saw ourselves getting closer to fulfilling our vision.

Why stop there? Next, we decided to work with John Travolta on a movie he and a few partners had been trying to make for quite some time called *Gotti*, based on the story written by John Gotti Jr. about his father. It is really a love story for his father. John Gotti Sr. was one of the last of the gentleman dons among mafia leaders. Of course, behind that persona he was a ruthless killer, and despite being a loving father and husband, he was not exactly the character portrayed in the film.

Travolta did an amazing job portraying him and showing how he evolved over time, eventually going to prison and dying there. The red-carpet event for *Gotti* was so big we had to rent two theaters in New York to hold all the attendees, which in-cluded several MoviePass contest winners and many celebrities, including 50 Cent. Of course, John Travolta and his wife, Kelly Preston, also in the movie, were there, flying in on Travolta's newly branded MoviePass private jet.

As I was entering the theater, I looked at my tickets and re-alized that I was sitting right next to Victoria Gotti, John Gotti's widow. Sitting next to her was this little guy who was obviously her protector, which made me slightly uncomfortable. I really didn't know how to react when watching the scenes in which Kelly Preston portrays Victoria throwing things and getting all upset.

It was another great MoviePass event and demonstrated our growth trajectory and our growing impact on the industry. At this point we had purchased 6.6 percent of the $5.5 billion in tickets sold in the first half of 2018 in the United States. But problems were looming. We were doing way too many things with too many irons in the fire. Besides producing films and investing in big events to raise awareness, we were creating and launching clever social stunts run by a company Ted had hired, the social media PR firm Jerry Media, with a very revealing handle, @fuckjerry. The company specialized in wild and thought-provoking social media posts and would eventually become known for producing the Fyre Festival documentary for Netflix.

Right around this time we received our first of several requests from the Federal Trade Commission (FTC) for information on our failure to supply new member cards in a timely manner and other complaints from customers. Many of those complaints were centered on our fraud prevention measures. Our head of product managed all of our responses, and the FTC was satisfied we were operating properly. Or so I was led to believe.

How could I have forgotten all those lessons I learned from Reed Hastings and Marc Randolph and Gregg Kaplan? They had taught me about focus and concentrating on doing, as Reed used to say, "that one thing that we can do better than anyone else." Instead, MoviePass was trying to do too many things at once. All of them were aimed at getting cash flow positive as soon as possible and before our funding would run out.

I have to admit that I failed to reach out for advice to a huge and valuable network of amazing advisors that the company had built. Our cadre of advisors included Thomas Tull from Legendary Pictures, Michael Ovitz, Shane Bliemaster, Jim Ramo, Hugh Pinero, and many others. Most had been brought on by the visionary founders of the company, Stacy Spikes and Hamet Watt.

I will always regret not taking advantage of the wealth of knowledge and help that these advisors could have provided. It reminds me of an executive offsite we had at Redbox. We hired the husband/wife duo of Clyde and Carolyn Lowstuter to help the leadership team of Redbox learn to be better leaders. One of the exercises appeared at first to make no sense. Clyde and his wife had strung a ninety-foot rope from tree to tree in a park and every three or four yards attached a tool to the rope. We were all blindfolded and led to the rope and told to hold on to the rope and move along until we discovered the solution to exit the course. Once we figured out the solution, we were told to whisper it in the ear of one of the instructors. After a good hour all but one of us had solved the puzzle and we all watched the one lone person still on the course.

The solution was essentially to ask one of the instructors for advice on how to solve the puzzle. One of our leaders had still not asked for that help. Despite this, he was one of the most inspiring and passionate and ultimately successful people I have ever worked with. But the lesson is, always ask for help or advice. I had failed to do this.

So I was on my own managing an incredible number of things—the endless efforts to reduce fraud, Bernadette's theater partnerships, partnerships with a company called Moocho to allow our app to secure babysitting and buy dinner or drinks, studio advertising partnerships and bounties, attempts to use social media and marketing to attract profitable subscribers who wouldn't overuse the service, and identifying scripts to produce. We were also trying to close the ill-fated Landmark Theatres deal and to buy Screenvision, the number two company in onscreen theater advertising.

And this was not an easy time for me personally. I had been having an affair and split from my wife, Zamora, who was shocked and devastated. After forty years of her full support I had abandoned her. I will always be grateful to her, but during this time there was constant arguing about how to resolve things in the divorce.

We also had our HR team organizing company events and launching team-building events. By June 2018 we had reached our peak of about eighty employees, mostly in New York, with about ten or eleven in Los Angeles focused on studio partnerships and other biz dev deals.

In the midst of all this, I went to Ted and showed him how in April and May we were able to reduce fraud by about 30 percent, which got us to an average usage of only 1.55 movies. I remember thinking that we were on the right track if we could continue to identify and eliminate fraud, attract a more casual user, and add revenue streams from advertising and partnerships. We might win the race before running out of money, which was becoming increasingly difficult to bring in. If Bernadette's team could continue to get 25 percent discounts on the costs of tickets and ideally sign up one of the three big chains, and if we could bring all those things together, we could become profitable and, more importantly, assist in the regrowth of the cinema and theater business and bring people back to watch independent films.

And then the proverbial shit hit the fan.

At the end of July, Paramount Pictures was releasing the new film *Mission: Impossible—Fallout*. When Sanjay shared with me our potential shortfall in funds that week, I knew we needed to do something or else the company would be unable to pay for tickets or employee salaries. The executive team had been testing a number of what we called "capped" plans that, while still generous, would greatly reduce our cash burn. But launching new plans would only help with new subscribers, while our burn was generated by around seven hundred thousand of our three million current subscribers. Among that seven hundred thousand were around five hundred thousand subscribers who had joined with an annual plan through Costco or directly with us.

So after discussing with the team, we decided on the following strategy: The first and most impactful decision would be to get more aggressive at reducing the amount of fraud. We had identified several hundred thousand subscribers who we believed might be sharing the card with friends and so were paying for one subscriber but buying tickets for two people. We were not sure who among this group was acting contrary to our terms and conditions, so we asked about 25 percent of them to change their account password. We did not block their accounts. They simply had to go to their account profile and enter a new password. We believed that if you were sharing your password with one or more friends, perhaps you would not reviolate our T&Cs. At the same time we stopped offering the Unlimited Program to new subscribers. All new subscribers no longer were able to join in the unlimited version but rather started with a "capped" plan. And we offered a large group of the annual subscribers a cash buyout or a conversion to a "capped" plan. Over the next three months, around 170,000 of the annual plan subscribers received full refunds of the unused portion of their year. Even so, we still spent over $10 million on *Mission: Impossible* tickets, which was around $3 million less than we might have spent.

What I didn't realize was that executing this set of moves was like pulling out the wrong piece from a wobbling Jenga tower. By Monday in the first week of August, Sanjay was calling and saying that Vantiv no longer would give us credit for a few days or a week as it had in the past, but now demanded a $5 million advance to be held on deposit. At the same time, Ted and our banker let us know that we had no money available.

What could we do? There were only two options: shut down or set a daily budget of how much we could spend and not go out of business. We were bringing in around $25 million in subscriptions and $2 million in advertising and partnerships with around $4 million in monthly operating costs, so we could spend about $5 million a week on tickets.

I chose the second option—hoping that I would find a new source for funding soon. I immediately sent an email to every one of our 3.2 million subscribers explaining that they could no longer count on MoviePass having every movie or showtime or theater available. I was interviewed in an endless number of news stories about the changes in availability, and if you lived in the United States and did not know that MoviePass was no longer the unlimited movie theater subscription service it had been, you had to be living under a rock. Simultaneously I instructed our team to remove the word *unlimited* from any of our communications and our website.

There were a lot of lessons to be learned from all of this—both the rise and the fall. First, if you have to operate at a negative margin for a time, it's best not to be owned by a public company. And second—there is such a thing as too much growth. We should have created a waiting list, instead of just accepting everyone, at least until we had worked out the fraud problems and the issues with the cinema industry and credit card companies.

As with all sinking ships, numerous employees started leaving for other jobs, and the existing team began an endless wave of complaints about my and my leadership team's failures. And thus began a year of Band-Aids, living within our means, driving customers mad, and losing over 2 million of our 3.2 million subscribers. Remember the funds that the credit card companies held on to? Well, we used that money to refund all but around ten thousand subscribers for their unused subscriptions.

To make matters worse, I received an email from an unknown person in the Middle East who claimed he had identified a weakness in our customer information storage and if I did not pay him $25,000 immediately, he would go to the press with the info. I was not in the mood for being extorted and I checked with our CTO, who said that this claim was unlikely. But I was shocked when the following week the press reported all this and once again the FTC and other government groups were all over us.

It turned out a third-party engineering team we had hired had copied a customer file onto an unsecured laptop. As far as I knew, no customer information was ever stolen, but the fact that it could have been and we had not responded quickly enough put us in the crosshairs of an FTC action. I was devastated by one piece of bad news after another. My best employees were leaving us, our money was drying up, our subscribers were asking for and receiving refunds or canceling, the press was crowing over our downfall, and my life seemed to be spiraling out of control. As if that wasn't enough, my kids were blaming me for the divorce, which was still not settled.

Toward the end of November, I couldn't handle it anymore, and I turned over leadership to Khalid and took a sabbatical. After sixty days, it was clear that he couldn't handle things either. He let people he never got along with go, alienated others, and did not solve the major issue of our software not fully canceling canceled subscribers. People who canceled their subscriptions during this time period continued to get billed because of a mistake in how our subscription billing company handled payments and cancellations. This looked very bad and was the beginning of our more serious problems with the FTC. I ended up coming back in February to try to fix the problems.

The next year was filled with subpoenas, requests for data and email, and lots of back and forth with the FTC. Ultimately, in January 2020 we filed for bankruptcy and faced numerous local and US government actions against the company and its leaders, including me. These took a long time to play out. The nightmare that began in August 2018 still had not run its course in October 2021. These were three-plus years I would never wish on my worst enemy and one of the hardest and most compelling set of lessons I have ever learned.

I had gotten caught up in all the frantic excitement. But I was forgetting the Buddhist teachings, that craving is the source for all pain and suffering, that all things must pass, and that frantic activity is not really real. I also learned that there are lots of people out there who actually want to see your business fail for their own selfish reasons. That really made me sad.

We were on our way to accomplishing the vision of transforming the movie business and giving people more reasons to see indie films, good stories made by passionate filmmakers, not just meaningless blockbusters.

My Buddhism allowed me to compartmentalize all these things and not have them totally destroy my view of life. I was able to bring some calm to it, to not have this failure be a pervasive thought in my mind from waking up to going to sleep again.

I think no matter what, all the way up until today, what I have learned is that all things change, life is filled with pain, and the only way to avoid that pain is to eliminate cravings for being popular, being rich, and being important.

I am left with my rich experience of life and a new wife who I am really in love with. And I have gained a unique perspective on the business of entertainment.

TAKEAWAY

The best intentions are not enough. Forgetting all the lessons and techniques and strategies you have learned is a path that can lead to failure. Losing focus and trying to do too many things at the same time increases the likelihood of losing and not having a strong family life foundation, which is not good for solving complex business challenges and proper execution of business objectives.

[11]

REFLECTIONS ON MY LIFE AND OUR FUTURE

The Buddha taught that everything is connected and that everything is constantly changing. That holds true in the past,
today, and in the future.

What will the future hold? One way to get a sense of what the
future might look like is to spend time in it. So let's join Carmen and Steven and their small family, who are media consumers
in the near future.

Steven is a cook at a local restaurant in a suburb of Omaha,
Nebraska, and his wife, Carmen, works in the finance department
of a retail clothing chain. They have two children: Isabel, who is
thirteen, and Ricky, who is eight.

Weekdays start with a whirlwind of activity, getting the kids
awake, fed, and prepared for school. The kids awaken to the warm
glow of a monitor next to each of their beds with soft music that
grows ever more intense. Once the system recognizes that the kids
are stirring, they hear Carmen's recorded voice saying, "Good
morning, I love you, time to get up."

This is followed by an outline of the upcoming day's activities and what they need to bring to school, plus a weather report with accompanying advice on clothing. Next comes a video of their teachers detailing what homework needs to be uploaded to the school website before leaving home.

This video ends with encouragement to get up and get dressed. The children move on to the bathroom and once there, as a reward for being a bit ahead of schedule, one of their favorite series, *SpongeBob at the Center of the Earth*, comes on the bathroom monitor. Each episode is only five minutes long and once the credits roll, Ricky and Isabel are moving to the kitchen for breakfast.

Steven is eating eggs and toast that he prepared himself and watching a holographic display above the table showing the news of the day. Using his right forefinger, he swipes left/right and up/down to choose what to watch. He settles on a story about the latest farming reports. He prides himself on getting the freshest locally grown produce for the restaurant where he works. He is hoping that one day the owner will sell him a piece of the restaurant, but he has been waiting five years now.

Carmen is still dressing upstairs and multitasking just like the kids—viewing the latest episode of *Dark Wine*, a Netflix series that Carmen and two of her work friends discuss and opine on every day at work during their regular meetings in their Meta re-creation of their office. What will happen next; why did Sophia dump Armando? It makes the hours working a bit more enjoyable. Netflix now offers a "non-bingeing," cliffhanger-laden viewing option that releases short episodes on either a Tuesday or Friday release schedule and is ideal for friends who want to watch at the same pace. Carmen chose this over the recently launched free advertising-supported

Netflix channel. As she watches the short program, she is also going over her agenda for the day, meetings, deliverables, and so on, as well as checking on the kids' school uploads.

Now she is moving fast as she hears a beep that tells her the driverless car waits outside for the kids. Everything—the car, the house, and all the equipment they use—is rented or part of a subscription. The need to own anything material is not even a thought for Steven and Carmen. There is the cultural recognition that all things are temporary, much like the Buddhist saying that all things change and nothing lasts very long. The biggest companies are those that manage these subscriptions and design life-encompassing programming based on your current earnings and your earning potential, proposing plans that you can afford.

Everyone has personal identification embedded under the skin near their wrists. This makes it possible to open your home, your office, your school, and your devices just by approaching them. No one needs a password.

Once out of the home, the family all don glasses that not only document what you see but also act as monitors and holographic projectors for anything you want to see or hear from the news, social media, episodic series, personal communications, or whatever. The kids head to school. As Isabel glances out the window, she sees monitors large and small all along the roadway all acknowledging her personally and presenting her with things to see. Since the car is moving at about fifty kilometers per hour, the screens along the road are acting in sequence.

Ricky is in the middle of editing the video short he is about to launch on FlickFlack, the new platform that is the rage of the day. FlickFlack has built-in special effects and animation along with a huge library of sound effects that make almost anyone into a creative genius. He has done four filming sessions, has brought in three different music backgrounds, and now is adding some special effects. Whew, he finishes and launches it just as they reach their school.

Meanwhile Steven's driverless car has arrived to take him to the market, where he can carefully and thoughtfully select produce and meats for the day's menu. Like his son, Ricky, Steven pulls up his menu of the day while in the car and begins to create a video for each new main dish showing ingredients and the prep process and cooking. He adds the right music theme based on the food type and has completed videos for three of the four dishes as the car pulls up to the market. He decides that once the video guide to the day's menu is completed, he will launch it at all monitors that are in or on an approach to a five-kilometer (yes, we have converted to the metric system) radius around the restaurant.

Carmen will work from home today. Between meetings, she will create a marketing video for the Chanel luxury handbag she bought herself as a gift last year that she now wants to sell. She will incorporate video and stills of the many good times she had with her girlfriends and husband that feature the bag. She has 150,000 Instagram followers and access to analytic platforms for reaching the right audience.

Isabel, too, like her savvy mom and equally smart brother, uses the "Find Your Fan" analytic platform dashboard when crafting and distributing her FlickFlack, TikTok, and Instagram posts to reach optimum viewers.

At lunch in the kitchen, Carmen flicks her fingers in midair to activate the monitor and settles in to watch the latest episode of her second-favorite series, *Vikings 2030*. But the screen erupts into a Godzilla-like character with Ricky's voice complaining loudly about not sending him access to his token wallet. He is desperate to purchase a non-fungible token (NFT) of the goal scored last night in the Berlin eSports World Cup and does not want to lose out to his archenemy Carl. Carmen quickly obliges by transferring enough tokens to Ricky for his acquisition.

Steven is navigating the farmer's market. His assistant, who met him at the market, is pushing a large cart next to him. He has opened his fruit and vegetable freshness and quality app in his smart glasses. As he focuses on the broccoli, up pops a list of vitamins and other characteristics of each bunch. He points out four bunches that meet his quality demands to his assistant. After an hour of this, he has enough of the ingredients for the day's meals. They both jump in a car to head to the restaurant's kitchen and during the half-hour ride, Steven completes the video of each meal and component along with calorie, sodium, and nutritional contents. His videos compare favorably to the best movie trailers you've ever watched, with a great soundtrack, special effects, and the sense of how much you will enjoy each meal.

The kids' classroom is filled with both physical and virtual monitors occupied by teachers from all over the world. The subject of biology is led by a young woman from the Congo, while math is taught by a recently accredited teacher in Boston. The classes allow Isabel and Ricky to interact with the teacher via text and voice to get clarification on subjects they aren't grasping, and the responses come from an in-depth machine learning and AI library of questions and answers. During the three breaks in the day, Ricky moves to an auditorium-style classroom where he launches a war game, while Isabel sits out on the lawn and video calls her best friend who is sitting a few feet away.

Meanwhile, Carmen's day is filled with metaverse meetings powered by Touchcast that re-creates settings with moving cameras and 3D virtual environments tailored to the purpose of the meetings. Documents have taken the form of a video introduction and short documentary. Another day of interacting with dozens of people and companies in multiple countries is close to being done.

Later that day, the kids leave school for training lessons. Ricky's soccer training is led in virtual reality by none other than Neymar Jr., the long-since-retired Brazilian soccer player. The interactive holographic lesson is just one of many lessons in all sports from Skillset, an Israeli company offering Masterclass for Sports. Isabel, meanwhile, is taking an Ultimate Fighting Champion (UFC) fighting skills class and feels like she is making lots of progress for a thirteen-year-old.

Later Steven returns home for an hour to have dinner with the family before heading back to the restaurant. Carmen and Steven do their best to enforce a "no media" hour so they can all talk and share the events of the day with each other. As usual, the kids are not jumping in. They keep glancing over at the various monitors around the dining area, wanting for the hour to end. Carmen starts off by sharing her day, as does Steven. There are many silent moments, but soon the hour is over and the kids race to their rooms.

Steven hugs Carmen and heads back to work. Carmen throws herself back on the couch and after a long pause, with one swipe of her hand in midair, brings up a screen showing the bids on her Chanel bag. Wow, 2,000 tokens bid. Her bottom line is 2,300, so she's almost there. Now she is sliding through the video messages from friends and work mates. Lastly, she sees a preview of tomorrow's episode of *Dark Wine*. What a day it has been.

Soon she is asleep. The kids, now done with schoolwork and communicating with friends, are settling down to watch a show. But which one? How do they choose from over one billion new pieces of content made available since yesterday? After browsing suggestions and scanning options for twenty minutes, they both give up and fall asleep, too. Maybe they should try the Katch Media app that identifies the genomic aspects of content and matches new series or FlickFlack clips to your own interests.

———

I HOPE YOU ENJOYED MY LITTLE STORY ABOUT THE FUTURE. IT stems from my observation of some big and pervasive trends. One, stories compel people's attention. Two, media is infiltrating everything in our lives. Three, soon everyone will be able to create compelling media. Four, that media is becoming much shorter. And five, the technologies for helping us to find the media that works for us are going to get better. Let's examine these trends, starting with stories and our compelling need to consume them.

From time immemorial, humans have loved a good story. Look at the cave paintings of animals and hunters in the caves of Lascaux and you can imagine the inhabitants of the cave sitting around a fire after eating what meager foods they had, listening to the hunters tell the story of the hunt. Perhaps a wounded bison came charging at them, and as they all ran, one of them bravely stood his ground and administered the death strike.

Stories became ubiquitous over the many thousands of years since then. And long before the birth of Jesus, storytellers began to put their stories in writing. Homer's *Odyssey* retells the story of the hard life of a hero struggling against all odds to finally win against the gods and all enemies.

Writing stories so they could be read by anyone evolved into live performances from a team of storytellers, and then, in the twentieth century, live performances began to be recorded on media. In the late part of the century, broadcast television, then cable, brought first dozens, then hundreds, and now tens of thousands of new shows telling stories from romance to adventure to horror and science fiction.

We still love exciting, compelling, gripping stories and characters. The volume of stories we have heard since adolescence has grown so dramatically over the last fifty years; it really takes a great storyteller to deliver something that feels even halfway original and different. Rising from the ashes, the flawed hero, the story of conquest, of ambition, of evil and good, the return of the down and out—we have heard them all.

The next stage in this flood of stories began in 2008, when Netflix launched streaming, quickly followed by many competitors including global companies like Amazon, Disney, Paramount, and HBO. More regional companies such as the Arab streamer Shahid and the Mexican streamer Bling also appeared.

When the pandemic hit in 2020, the world suddenly had to spend many more hours at home and not commuting to work for eight-hour workdays. Streaming became the go-to affordable and convenient time-filler and entertainer. At the end of 2020, Netflix surpassed two hundred million paying households, Disney+ grew to over a hundred million subscribers in less than a year, and Paramount+ and many others added tens of millions of subs.

Part of what is driving all of this streaming is the vast increase in places to consume content. Smartphones have reached six billion people. Entertainment is no longer restricted to sitting in a theater or in front of a television. Most of us humans now have almost twenty-four-hour-a-day access to entertainment. When Reed Hastings, Netflix CEO for many years, was asked, "What is your biggest competitor?" he responded, "Sleep." And he was right.

As I referenced in the story of Carmen and Steven and their children, content will soon be everywhere: your smart glasses, smartphone, wrist-held monitors, media panels along roads and walkways, embedded in the ground, in floors, in ceilings, in self-driving cars, and so on. And it will all be completely aware and dynamic based on who is present. This dynamic will affect not just viewing but creation as well. We will all incorporate communicating in more and more sophisticated media ourselves. And that applies not just for business or entertainment but for connecting with friends and family as well.

Even as we generate demand for far more media, we—amateurs, not professional video creators—will be creating much of the media we consume.

The ten top media companies such as Netflix, Disney, and Amazon are spending a combined $130 billion plus a year on new content, producing over fifty thousand new TV episodes and over seven thousand full-length movies yearly. But that's still not enough to satisfy our voracious demand for media.

Meanwhile, technology, equipment, and storytelling technique have become better understood and practiced for a rapidly increasing number of creators. With an iPhone today, you can script, produce, and distribute content superbly, reaching niche or mass audiences. We are at the beginning of a true renaissance in media and story creation encouraged by the ability for almost anyone to create and distribute content without the gatekeepers of the past who decided what was worth distributing.

As a result, the volume of well-made content is soaring, with tens of millions of new entertainment pieces released monthly worldwide. Content creation, from filming to editing to special effects to story to acting, has become almost the entire world's passion and capability. Just look at the billion or so TikToks being created every week, or the billion or so YouTube videos. Many TikTok media creators have tens of millions of followers. Our culture, not just in Western countries but worldwide, is now one where everybody is making videos and even series from their smartphones and distributing them from content platforms to billions of voracious consumers.

Even as the content proliferates, the individual pieces of media are getting shorter.

Busy consumers are multitasking for work, family, and entertainment, all at the same time. University researchers estimate that the average person's attention span has dropped over the last ten years to eight seconds. No longer can viewers sit still for two hours for a full-length film, even though they are quite happy to sit for six hours bingeing on episodes of *Stranger Things*. But even thirty-minute series episodes are becoming tedious. The future — Carmen and Steven's future, as well as everyone else's — is one-, two-, five-, and ten-minute episodes of amateur-made content that fits our more and more niche interests. But just as when we sat around the fire listening to the master storyteller, we still want fully developed characters that we can fall in love with or care about and follow their journeys through life—just told in shorter chunks.

Binge watching will continue to be a popular way to consume content, but I believe we will see a resurgence in episodic viewing. Since James Fenimore Cooper created what we know as the "cliffhanger," it has served as an important ingredient in storytelling. These shorter pieces will incorporate cliffhangers at the end of each episode, with a wait time to see how the cliffhanger gets resolved. The benefit for both the viewer and content creator is that during those intervals, if the content is compelling, audiences will expand because of fans talking about what will happen next. There won't be the concern that a listener might be on an earlier episode and you could give away important elements.

The challenge for the future may be more about finding something to view without working too hard at it—finding something that makes you feel like that was a good use of the time. Of course, the technologies that help match content to a viewer have a long and checkered history. Personal recommendations have historically resulted in consumption. But because the recommender may be overselling or lacking an understanding of the nuances of taste, those recommendations often result in a failure to deliver value to the viewer.

Basic algorithms such as collaborative filtering place an individual in a "mentor group" and assume that if you have liked many series at the same level as others in your group, you will probably enjoy seeing media that others in your group enjoyed. But with the rise of artificial intelligence, the technologies that determine what content we consume and create will become smarter and smarter, home in on what we are interested in, and filter through billions of options. We will learn to trust these technologies to serve us, just as we count on Google Maps to get us from one place to another.

Now that almost anyone has the tools and the apps that assist storytelling through media, advertisers that once counted exclusively on agency creatives have now turned to crowdsourcing and crowd creation by their fans, rendering studios and distributors of content far less important. Everyone is a content creator. The platforms and the embedded analytics perform all marketing functions, and those platforms all include revenue components ranging from product placement to ad banners to charging for access or products.

Theaters will become gathering places for big social events like e-sports tournaments, binge-watching whole series on the big screen, and telecasts of live sporting events, filling the theater with shouts and cheers.

In the near future, all of our lives will be completely filled with media: creating media, consuming media, sharing media. Video and similar content is filling almost every crack in time and assisting almost everything we do, as it did for Steven when shopping for the best ingredients for his menu, and teaching us, as it did for Ricky training for soccer. It is a medium for communication among friends, family, and strangers; it is also entertainment, but the lines between messaging, selling, and learning are blurring.

There will still be services like Netflix, but the people who make content professionally will follow the market and make five-minute segments, consumable anywhere. The innovation will be, how do we create a natural place to stop? Commercials will keep getting shorter and will be created in much shorter segments.

There will be product integration to help generate revenue from all this media. Like Amazon, companies that produce and pay for stuff will be making money on other opportunities generated by having your attention. They will use media to build an audience, then make a profit from it in some other way.

I see this as upending the whole professional side of the business, as professional creators will create a much smaller percentage of the hours viewed. Lots of those folks will have to figure out a different way to make money and use their craft. When you make everyone a filmmaker, that disrupts the whole system. The fuel is people hoping to create the big score, to become one of the profitable video makers on TikTok or YouTube or whatever comes next. People vying to become the next big deal will create an incredible flood of content.

That's a vision for the future within a certain frame of reference with a focus on media and entertainment. But I have learned about a lot more than entertainment in my career. Since you have gotten to the end of my life story so far, I want to share two other things: what I learned about business, and what I learned about life.

Over the course of my fifty years in business I've learned many lessons. I learned a lot the hard way—I hope you've seen that with my narrative about the many failures and challenges I faced. But I've also learned from observing others, and I'm sure I still have much more to learn even now.

One crucial insight is this: Identifying *exactly* what you want to accomplish in business is critical. Even knowing that your goals will surely change, focusing on the vision and blocking out distractions is important.

I have learned that building a company is, above all, building a team, and that team needs to be as diverse as possible. To learn the most and accomplish the most, you will benefit from people with diverse backgrounds: gender, race, class, education, and people with origins all over the planet. As Clyde Lowstuter taught me, as a leader you need to understand what motivates each of your team members and how to offer that reward to them if you can, and if they deliver. Is that reward money, respect, more time, or something different and unique? It depends on the person.

Surrounding yourself with constructive, smart, and caring people is important, becoming an expert in the business you are in is important, persevering through obstacles both small and existential is important, but far and away more important is loving, and I do mean loving, what you are doing. Ideally you should be waking up each day, bouncing out of bed excited to face the decisions and the creativity that greets you as you build your idea into a business.

Remember the lesson of Tinkerbell. An entrepreneur is always tinkering, trying various combinations of variables until that fabled hockey stick performance appears with the ideal combination.

Don't grow too slowly or you will lose your teammates and investors; don't grow too fast or you will overwhelm the systems and capacity of your team. Communicate excessively, care about the well-being of others, design a product or service that truly improves on what exists, and ensure a path to being profitable.

As I write these words, I know I have succeeded in many of these skills and miserably failed in others. I have even learned a skill and then later completely forgot what I had learned. The key to it all is passion for what you are doing. That passion will guide you in overcoming any shortfall you might have when setting out.

But business is business. What has all this taught me about life?

As an adherent of Buddhist philosophy, I can only speak for myself. One of my strongest tenets is to respect that you may have a completely different set of beliefs than others do, and that is fine. I will never criticize nor demean you. We all must come to our own conclusions.

Over the course of these many years in life, in start-ups, in failures, and in family and relationships, I would have had to be blind and incoherent not to have learned a few lessons. Probably the most important is that everything changes. What was good goes bad, and what was bad becomes good. What worked before doesn't work now, and vice versa. As Richard Thaler explained, people do not always act logically or in their best interest. Even so, I have seen that all ideas can succeed if executed properly and that no one knows much about the future, especially the interaction among all the innovations that people come up with.

I have also come to the sad conclusion that my way has not been the best way. I should have slowed down, done more complete due diligence on the pros and cons of who and what to work on. What I was right about is that it is more important to get started down a path than to sit and wait for the perfect moment. We learn so much from trying that no amount of time spent evaluating can be better than the experience and understanding you get from doing.

In my experience, the best life is one where work and family and everything else are intertwined. The theory that you can create a work/life balance where work ends and life starts is a myth, a false direction. It is much better to enjoy work and know that life and work are constantly interacting with each other. It is also important to try to test new ideas, new friends, new products, and new everything. Expand your exposure, and while becoming a loyal customer of a product, do not be lazy and fail to test the competition. Constant exposure to the new will teach you a lot.

The beauty of meditation is that it gives your mind time to think through your own meaning of life. For me, as simple as it might sound, the most important goals are to have children, that those children have their own children, and to, in your own way, make the world a little bit better than it is. Your job is to be good and kind and to help others.

As you pursue your own ambitions of success and disruption and creation and entertainment, I hope these words can help you realize your dreams.

Never stop tinkering. You never know what you might discover.

ACKNOWLEDGMENTS

Marc Randolph, for teaching me to tinker.

Reed Hastings and Ted Sarandos, for making Netflix a household word.

Patty McCord, for teaching me about inclusiveness and diversity.

Gregg Kaplan, for showing me how to run a company.

Clyde Lowstuter, for teaching me how to be a leader.

Mary Leonard, for showing me how to run a big team.

Chris Kelly, for giving me an opportunity.

Sanjay Puri, for sticking by me.

Khalid Itum, for his energy.

Brian Rady, for teaching me about process.

Acknowledgments

Tim Hale, for teaching me about the importance of customer relationships.

TK Arnold and Tom Adams, for providing great insight to the entertainment industry.

Ken Sterling and the wonderful team at BigSpeak, for their guidance and support.

Ned Siegel and Dr. Raphael Nagel, for their friendship and welcoming me into a new dimension in my career.

Moshe Shapoff, for demonstrating international goodwill and peace in this world.

Jacques Achsen, for introducing me to Vipassana Buddhism.

Carmen Franko, Steven Saltzman, Carolin Jauss, Yuval Rabin, Noam Hachmon, Jakub Kokoszka, Andrew Tight, and Sharon Meusher, for your dedicated partnerships.

Alex Call and Brian Price, for getting me started on this book.

Josh Bernoff and Carolyn Monaco, for showing me how to write.

Zamora, for making all my ventures possible.

My mom who, along with my dad, brought us to California and showed my brother and me the world.

My brother Mark who, as my partner, kept the engine running and was the first to add business lines to our video stores.

Joaquin, Paloma, Emiliano, and Genesis, for being the lights of my life.

Sandra, for changing my life and creating a spiritual joy.

INDEX

Index

Index